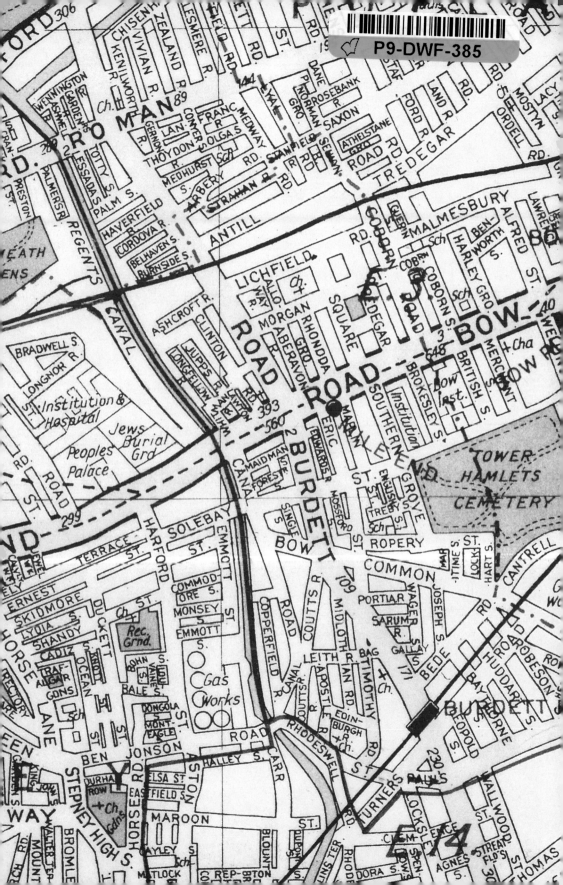

Terence Stamp

STAMP ALBUM

BLOOMSBURY

First published 1987
Copyright © 1987 by Terence Stamp

Bloomsbury Publishing Ltd, 4 Bloomsbury Place, London WC1A 2QA

British Library Cataloguing in Publication Data
Stamp, Terence
Stamp album.
1. Stamp, Terence   2. Actors — Great
Britain — Biography
I. Title
792'.028'0924   PN2598.S7/

ISBN 0–7475–0032–0

Designed by Newell and Sorrell Design Ltd
Phototypeset by Falcon Graphic Art Ltd
Wallington, Surrey
Printed in Great Britain by
Butler & Tanner Ltd, Frome, Somerset

'People like us don't do things like that,' said Tom Stamp firmly when his teenage son Terence began to show an interest in acting.

In this enchanting memoir Terence Stamp looks back with warmth and humour to a London East End childhood which began in the blazing glare of the Blitz. He was the first grandchild of two warring Cockney clans – the Stamps and the Perrotts – whose affections for the blue-eyed infant united them in a grudging truce. With father away at sea (torpedoed; his hair turned white overnight), Terence had no rivals for a mother's and a grandmother's love, and that, he thought, was as it should be.

The author's vivid memories take the reader back to the annual hop-picking holiday in Kent and with him as he battles for a place in the local grammar school. 'You would make a good manager of Woolworth's,' predicted one teacher, but that is not what 'our Tel' had in mind. At thirteen Terence enters the mysteries of sexual initiation in the laundry room of a convalescent home under the expert and energetic guidance of Nurse Grace. We watch the future film star 'urging' on his height, sporting a Dayton roll-collar shirt as worn by Dean Martin, supplementing his income as a newspaper delivery boy – always waiting for Gene Tierney to walk into his life.

It is patently clear from curtain-up that Terence Stamp is a born story-teller. The eloquent and witty delights of his *Stamp Album* capture an English childhood that has gone for ever.

FOR TOM AND ETHEL

CONTENTS

One

WITHIN
BOW BELLS

Above: Early holiday snap of Tom and Ethel

I always loved my mother to excess. When the first bomb of the Second World War dropped on Bow Cemetery, unmindful of the young prince still being breast-fed in a nearby street, my dad, Tom, signed himself back into the Merchant Navy, leaving my mum, Ethel, her wedding licence, with its Edward VIII stamp still uncreased, without her man. Except for me, that was. I became Dad's understudy for the duration of the War. Not that I had any complaints. A discerning spectator might have observed that I came almost made to measure for the role, even to the ear-length sideboards I was born with. These appendages which accompanied my mop of black hair caused much clucking between the two families gathered around the maternal bed, regarding one another like a set of Montagues and Capulets who'd ended their feud but were not at all sure they had done the right thing.

During the winter of '38 when Ethel was carrying me, she had the habit of wetting her finger and fixing Dad's long sideburns into shape. The nurses at Bancroft Road Maternity Hospital did much the same to me, so instead of seeing a 'fluffed-up' head like all the other newcomers, my relatives came upon a 'little old man', complete with parting and Victorian hairstyle, peering out from my mother's side. My Auntie Julie, who was to become my godmother, thought it 'romantic', but as the first grandchild of both families, Ethel being the eldest Perrott and Tom the Stamps' firstborn, both Cockney clans were only too pleased to endow me with anything special. I suppose it was special that I was ever born at all considering the amount of prejudice in the East End at that time, when even families who occupied upstairs rooms were looked down on by ground-floor dwellers. By rights my parents should have been kept apart by the territorial pecking order: Bow, my mother's home, with its E.1 postal district, within the sound of its famous bells, was more central and therefore more desirable than Poplar E.14 where the Stamps hailed from. Poplar was near the docks; it came complete with reputed prostitutes and opium dealers, and was bordered by Hackney Marshes, that well-known spawning ground of criminal types ever since Dick Turpin hit the road. I was too young for this nonsense to go anywhere but over my head, and grew up loving all four grandparents and both their houses. But the Perrotts did regard the Stamps as common, and Granny Stamp, who was said to pawn anything to get a drink, including her children's shoes, was considered shocking.

I asked my dad if there had been any truth to the rumours that he went barefoot as a child. He admitted, 'I did try it, but it was too hard.' He had come across a discarded pair of ladies' button-up high-heeled boots, in which he'd gaily galloped over the cobbled streets until they wore out. My mum told me he had often been without shoes because he couldn't resist his mother's charm when she'd asked for them. He'd spent much of his school-time indoors at home, ashamed to go out. Hc always read and wrote slowly. My own preoccupation with beautiful shoes probably stems from Dad's lack of them.

The Stamps were brought up to regard the Perrotts as a snooty lot, well above themselves. All of which naturally only heightened Tom's ardour for Ethel Esther, or Et as she was called. To him she must have appeared as an anointed Queen. Her father, Alfred, was a successful man, with a regular job in the kitchens of the main postal sorting-office at St Paul's. Ethel worked in the City, and was engaged to Harry Baker, the son of a shopowner, with a diamond ring to prove it. Both families had traditionally used the September hop harvest as a working holiday. Even at New Barns Farm, Yalding, where the hoppers were billeted in huts, the English preoccupation with hierarchy found its way. At one end of the Common were the small corrugated-iron huts housing the gypsies or diddicoys and the really rough; at the other end were the slightly bigger brick huts and 'the posh'! God knows when this class structure was established, but I never witnessed any change in territory – well only once, during the War when we were evacuated early in summer, and occupied one of the bigger tin huts midway on the Common. I liked it. I liked the sound the rain made on the roof at night.

My father was a handsome man. My mother said he reminded her of Spencer Tracy, although I'm sure he'd have much rather been compared with Cagney. (I asked the great Jimmy to sign his biography for Dad one Christmas. He was really chuffed.) I've always felt my dad had one of the best heads I've ever seen. All my life it gave me satisfaction just to look at him and watch the seasons of his face. Although I and my brothers have been considered 'lookers' at some time or other, none of us really had it like Tom. It seemed his physical attributes were divided between us. Ethel, like all the others, was taken by his charms, although it can't have been an easy wooing.

Above: Dad was always a Cagney fan

Tom and Ethel first met in the aphrodisiac hopfields. It hadn't been love at first sight. He liked taking the rise out of everybody; his clothes never matched or fitted and he looked scruffy. But Tom bewitched her brother and sisters, drawing cartoons and sketches of Popeye for them. They sang his praises to Ethel, and he was soon walking out with her on Sunday afternoons, promising to write when he went back to sea. It didn't take long for my grandmother to realise who the pencilled envelopes were coming from and they disappeared into her apron pocket as soon as she found them. Ethel's eleven-year-old sister Julie started waiting for the postman's tap and hid each letter for her when it was pushed under the front door. Home on shore leave, Tom sent a young mate of his, George Canham, to call on Julie. Although Julie wasn't allowed out with boys, this was the signal that Tom was waiting in the Velocipede (Velos–Floss) pub around the corner.

Soon came the day when Ethel broke her engagement with Harry Baker. He was so upset that he threw the ring she returned down the drainhole outside Number 96 Canal Road, where she was living at the time. Ethel's parents weren't too pleased either! And there was talk of getting the Borough to come and retrieve the diamond.

It was not Kate, the fearsome Aries in the size 2 shoes, but Alf, Ethel's father, who first saw the substance of Tom and perceived it was a real love match. A strong bond developed between the two men when Tom became his son-in-law.

When war broke out in '39, it was Alf who advised Tom to go back into the Merchant Navy – 'before they stick you in the Army. That's really the pits.' He'd served his time in the Great War. Tom took the advice, but Ethel (year of the Tiger, sun in Leo) never really believed that was the only reason. 'You prefer the sea to me,' was a remark typical of her possessiveness, although she told me that when they first met she hadn't wanted anything to do with him; it just happened 'in spite of herself'. It was as if Tom had drawn her to him by the very strength of his longing.

They were married on Boxing Day in '36. Dad bought himself a black Crombie overcoat for thirty bob down Petticoat Lane and they spent their honeymoon in Pitsea.

Dad gave up the sea as promised. In the Merchant Navy he had been a stoker or 'donkey man' and he got a job as a delivery boy with a hat shop, opposite the cigarette kiosk in Bond Street. Five shillings a week, with use of the bike, which he used to cycle to and from Poplar every day to save bus fares. Their first home was a couple of rooms in 12 Hudson Buildings, Prestons Road, just past the Blackwall Tunnel entrance towards the Isle of Dogs. It was this flat I returned to when Ethel came out of Bancroft Road Maternity Hospital. I didn't like it. I fretted, I cried, I moaned, I caught colds. It was only when I was wheeled in my pram to Kate's house at 96 Canal Road that all my symptoms stopped instantly. It seems I always had a strong sense of knowing what I liked. Kate I liked. That I adored her is nearer the truth. They say the Prophet Muhammad was brought up by his grandparents, and I can think of no greater blessing for a new spirit than to have their close presence. I've often heard about the exchange between a new soul on its way in and an old soul on its way out, which is as may be. All I know is that being with Gran Perrott was bliss for me. So, when Dad went back to sea, Mum returned to Canal Road, the Blitz began and I was in heaven.

Above: Mum and Dad on honeymoon

Left: Me with Granny Kate

Catherine Willmore had moved into Canal Road three years after she married Alfred Perrott in 1915. It was a quaint little street a stone's throw from Burdett Road Market with two-thirds of the houses, down to the wooden bridge, a single row looking across at the canal. When Kate moved in milk was purchased directly from cows at the dairy a few doors away and local hobbadies still swam in the murky water, but by the late Thirties the municipal pool in Victoria Park had opened and the Regent's Canal had become used to a quiet life. It wasn't much to shout about, being all of seven or eight feet across, but for someone such as myself with a crustacean predisposition the mere presence of an urban river, albeit man-made, on my doorstep was a kind stroke of providence. Apparently Kate had always had a soft spot for Alf's younger brother Dave, who was the rascal of the family. Whether Kate was one of those girls that liked guys who were trouble, or whether it was a natural bonding, is hard to say but in any case she settled for the less flamboyant Alf. It proved to be a combustible partnership, as is right with a mating of two Aries. Furious rows would be followed by the household gearing itself for another addition. There were nine pregnancies in all; four died very young and a fifth, the angelic Millie, died mysteriously of 'unknown foreign bodies' when only two, leaving Ethel Esther, Julie, Harry and the youngest, Maude Catherine, the seventh child of a seventh child. All, with the exception of Ethel, were born at 96 Canal Road.

I only knew my Grandfather Perrott when he had one arm. Some time before I arrived on the scene he had grown fed up with wearing a collar and tie to go to work, so he had given up his job as a chef and had found employment with the Stepney Electricity Board where he happily went to work collarless, sporting a white scarf. Dreadful conjunctions must have been in the sky for Alf and Kate that July of 1931. Little Millie, running across the living-room at the sight of her father, stopped short, smiled wistfully at him and fell down. She had gone before he picked her up. Telephoning his guvnor from the phone box outside the Mile End Odeon, to ask if he might take his holiday early, Alf was cut short by the answer, 'Fuck you, Perrott, I'm sick to death of you guys changing your holidays, be here on time tomorrow or you're fired.'

That morning the power was accidentally left on and, at five forty-five a.m., when Alf opened a terminal box at Bethnal Green for cleaning, he received the voltage through his body for a full four

Above:
Grandad Perrott
after the accident

Right: Millie

minutes before a mate with rubber boots came and kicked him clear. Alf was the colour of a new penny for a month and when they removed the dressing his arm came off with the bandages. Such were the hardships that forged the lives of my ancestors. Not that it stopped him doing much. He made me wooden tanks and other toys at Christmas and I sat on his lap at the LEB switchboard, his compensation job, clasping his empty sleeve and as secure in his one arm as any other grandchild in two.

The Stamp patchwork was cut from a different cloth. Granny Stamp's house in Poplar was so tiny that it might have come directly out of *Hansel and Gretel*, except there was no gilt on this gingerbread. When Tom was a boy in Mills Grove there was no bread at all, let alone ginger. Things had improved considerably by the time I was shown off there every other Sunday. Sometimes I would be taken to see my great-grandmother who was in a home, but it was the visits to Number 28 I remember most clearly. The house had a completely different smell from Canal Road; the interior was so small that whatever odour was dominant swamped each floor. In the winter we would bang the heavy black knocker, extricate the key which hung on a piece of string behind the vertical letterbox and let ourselves into the dark passage. At the far end down a step would be Gran sitting in a pool of light by the stove in her wooden armchair. The aroma from the glass of ale would hiss up the narrow hall, as she drew the hot poker from the coals and plunged it into the pint glass. In the summer the front door was always open, held immobile by a cast-iron doorstop. Then the odour would be the spicy fumes of her favourite snuff to which she was addicted, and which as I grew bigger I was proud to buy for her from the nearby shop, Hollocks (you can imagine what she called it when they wouldn't accept any more credit), a ha'p'orth in a neat twist of newspaper.

Nanny Stamp had started life as Mary Allen, her parents having come over from Wicklow in Ireland. She had thick Irish curls, black as jet, and would burst into song at the drop of a milk stout. This 'Primrose of Poplar' as she was known was hard to resist.

Charles Henry Stamp (my dad only spoke of him as 'the ole man' and Granny always referred to him as 'Charlie Harry') reputedly had family who owned dairy shops in Devon, but Harry, the black sheep, had left home and chosen the sea. He was good-looking, small and wiry, but with the high cheekbones and

Above: 'Charlie Harry' and the 'Primrose of Poplar'

forehead that predominate in our family. He must have been tough, for he had that gentleness that only the truly strong possess. His eyes the palest of blue, like faded denim, were inherited by my dad and my brother Chris. I remember his glance being steady, as if he were looking through clear water. He had had to fight two of Mary Allen's brothers, they being Catholic and very protective, before he could walk out with her. I understand that he dropped them like stones, one after the other. Nobody ever heard him raise his voice to her although it is obvious from the few photos of her when young that she was a right handful. She had such astonishing spirit it must have been impossible not to forgive her transgressions. Even in the face of destitution, the Irish eyes would twinkle, there would be a sigh of 'Ah! God's good!', and the voice that brought a hush to all the saloon bars in the neighbourhood would start to sing.

Tom had three younger brothers and two sisters. The life was hard for all of them, being more dinner-times than dinners. It wasn't until recently, when Tom and I started meeting regularly for afternoon coffee, that I really began to learn about his early life. Tom, having spent a lifetime in pubs and bars around the world, had an appreciation for a 'good room', and the Soda Fountain at Fortnum and Mason's, before the owner mysteriously paid a small fortune to have Hugh Casson Associates turn it into an airport caff, fitted the bill. I would get there before the afternoon tea rush and get the old 'number one' table in the corner, with a banquette seat and a prime view of the room. Tom would arrive, order a strong black with hot milk separate, and proceed to wisecrack about the eccentrics that frequented the Fountain before it committed suicide. After a bit of prodding he could be drawn out on his early life.

All his brothers and sisters loved their mother, but looked forward to their dad's homecomings, when regular meals appeared, coal burned cheerfully in the grate, and new outfits were purchased for all of them. When he went back to sea he always left his wife money to look after them and herself. Their mother soon spent it. Clothes would vanish from the cupboard and food became scarce. Tom spent hours scavenging under the stalls in Chrisp Street Market for spec fruit and the odd chocolate overlooked in the discarded boxes. He was brought up mostly by his Aunt Ninna who lived nearby. His system must have adapted to a lack of warm clothing – he was always turning down the central heating system and lowering the temperature of the Aga cooker later in life – but it was clear that his earlier existence had been motivated by keeping warm and finding enough to eat.

My dad had a great sense of humour, and folks who knew him as a boy said he was always a joy to be with, but I'm sure this seeing the funny side of things came about to counter the harrowing reality. He had me in stitches when he told me the story of the time the bailiffs took possession of the house in Mills Grove. Tom had come home from school to find the front door padlocked. Not knowing what to do, he just sat on the doorstep and waited. A man arrived and took him into care. By the time his dad had docked, found a lodger who would pay rent in advance, settled some of the debts and located his kids, Tom didn't want to go home. His father had to drag him out of the institution, Tom vocalising his disbelief at being taken away from his own bed with clean sheets, blankets, and three meals a day, including an egg for breakfast. 'Where's this boxer [the lodger] gonna go? In our room? There's four of us in it already.'

As Tom suspected, they had to sleep in the passage until the landlord's debt was completely paid and the boxing champ moved on. He always chuckled at the memory of his youngest brother, Barny, who on coming home from school every day would run indoors to look into the oven. 'All that ever came out of there was a spider!'

The picture that emerged of his mother was of an irresponsible free spirit, unequipped to raise a family. When Tom was fifteen and no longer required to attend school, his mother took him to a nearby café where she charmed the owner into giving him a job. 'This is my Tommy. He's a good boy, a really hard worker. Why don't you take him on for a few days? I'll really miss him at home, he's such a help – see how he does.'

At the end of his first day's work, the owner's wife asked Tom if he wouldn't mind just throwing away those steamed apple puddings that hadn't been sold. Dad's face was a picture, re-creating the incredulity he'd felt at that moment. Not wanting to seem stupid, fearful of making one misstep, but at the same time not really believing this food was actually being thrown into a dustbin, and that his hand was to do it, he said, 'D'you mean away, throw it away?'

'Yes, that's right, dear.'

'D'you, d'you mind if I take 'em home? My brother Barny is partial to an apple pud.'

Tom recalled his brothers' faces at his laden entrance, and his mother giving him a wink and saying, 'Perhaps there'll be some steak and kidney puds thrown out tomorrow, eh Tom?'

I think Tom had the kind of relationship with his dad that I would have liked to have had with mine but didn't. He told me a story about how he first went to sea. Dad was sixteen the first time Harry took him aboard. The ship was in the East India Dock and Harry was returning some laundry – *Dobi*, he called it – to other crew members. It seems he did odds and ends like this to make a few extra shillings. Taking Tom to his cabin, he left him alone there while he delivered the washing. Tom, poking around, discovered behind a little curtain above the bunk a food stash with a huge piece of cheese, 'Big, like in a shop.'

When Harry returned, he quizzed him on it.

'That's where we keep our extra grub.'

By the time they had left the ship Tom had decided he wanted to go to sea. He asked his father how to go about it.

'Oh, just see the fella at the shipping office and sign on.'

Tom went to sign on immediately. It was only when he was asked his age that he discovered he was too young. When he took this point up with Harry, his dad said, 'Oh, yeah, well wait till next year and then tell them you're older.'

Which he did. He was always a year older on his seaman's book, but he told me, 'It was probably the ole man's way of making sure it was what I really wanted to do.'

When I had left school, and my brother Chris was coming up for fourteen, Dad starting taking him out on the tug he was driving. Chris was obviously having a great time on the river. I envied those trips, but Dad never asked me along.

Dad could not have had a room of his own, or even a space, until after the War when we moved to Chadwin Road in Plaistow. It was in the yard, which I suppose was designed as a garden but the only time anything ever grew there was the year after the sewage cover was flooded off and the yard was so deluged with a variety of unmentionables that tomato plants and all sorts of things sprang up. Anyway, in these few miserable square yards Dad built himself a lean-to shed against the fence which separated us from Mrs

Roland and her turquoise macaw. This side of the yard now consisted of the outside loo, the coal bunker and Dad's corrugated-iron masterpiece. Later, when we got our first telly, he nailed a piece of wood above the door and chalked on it, 'The Ponderosa'! Into his ranch-house went every tool, nail, screw, piece of wire, string or wood that he had ever acquired. There was no electric light; it was completely black when the door was closed, with only a little space to stand in front of the bench. But Dad seemed to spend hours in there. Christ knows what he got up to, but as I got older and being a fellow Cancerian, with a special awareness of space and a need for privacy, I often recalled a remark he made about his first voyage when he had been shown into a room amidships filled with bunks and hammocks. The mate had pointed to a spot on the floor and said, 'Just stash your kitbag over there, lad, it'll be all right there.' But it was his own hammock, and the hard work involving all hours was balanced with regular meals and voyages to places other men his age never dreamed of. He wasn't unhappy to be away from home.

Visiting Granny Stamp by bus on my own every other Sunday, I explored the whole house. Except for the living-room and scullery, all the rooms were used as bedrooms. They were so small and dim that it was hard to move around in what little area was uncluttered. Two objects fascinated me in the front room: one was a stuffed bird, the other an arrangement of dried flowers; both were under domed glass cases. I asked my Uncle Barny what he called them.

'Them,' he said.

'That's all? Just them?'

'Well, them in there.'

Their dad had brought them home from one of his trips; they had a French name which none of the kids could pronounce. All the rooms had sentimentalised holy pictures of Jesus and Mary with exposed glowing hearts. Rosaries hung under them on the wall. Those rooms were not places to play. I amused myself outside in the back. I had been intrigued by the back yard ever since Dad had told me the tale of an apple seed he had planted which had grown up to be a pear tree. There was no evidence of anything growing at all when I began my investigations; it hadn't occurred to me that Dad might have been pulling my leg and I was always on the look-out for any strange transmutations. Number 28 was the last house on the east side of Mills Grove, but the corner position was taken up by a sweet factory whose high side wall ran the length of the yard, shutting out most of the light from the living-room and overshadowing the one attempt at a flower-bed. This grim obstacle did have an advantage. When Mary, Dad's sister, worked there as a girl, she would open the factory window on dim evenings and tip a tray of toffees out for Barny and John, the two youngest brothers, waiting in the garden to pick up the loot.

In the Perrott household the garden was always tended by Alf. One of their houses in Canal Road had a grapevine which grew through the wall into the scullery. Even after Alf went to live in the sanatorium the garden in Barking Road was kept up. When I lived there I had a rabbit named Pieshop who did the lawn and I made it my business to collect seeds and transplant anything promising I came across on wasteground. When the family left the East End for good the garden was still sporting lupins and Black Prince hollyhocks that Granny Kate and I had put there.

Mills Grove was the opposite. It was urban decay, with nature excluded. The only point of interest was a brick shed taking up most of the patch; it was so filled with debris that even when I wrenched the door open I couldn't get inside. One time after Gran had nipped around the corner to the St Leonard's Arms with her jug, I climbed a wall and up on to the roof of the shed. After devoting my attention to the remnants that wind up on a flat roof, I saw a weed growing out of the low parapet which ran around the edge of the building. It had pink flowers and usually grew on the bomb-damaged sites. So common, in fact, that I had never before given it a second glance. This particular plant, so solitary and bright, growing directly out of two bricks, set itself apart from its dank surroundings. I tried to get it out, intending to replant it in Kate's garden, but it broke off in my hands.

The next time I visited Granny Stamp I clambered back on to the roof and found the plant flowering once more. I counted the bricks from the corner of the parapet, marked the two it was growing between and broke it off again. In October, when I longed for a big toy fort and soldiers ready early for Christmas in the shop windows next to Jolly's the grocer in St Leonard's Road, I climbed on to the roof for a third time and, to my astonishment, there was the Fire Weed growing stronger than ever, with white fluffy seeds waiting to be blown off by the wind. I was so excited by the magical powers of this little flower that I couldn't wait to tell Dad about it, but he wasn't really interested. My dad only began to open up to me when I was in my late twenties. But maybe this is commonplace? I know in the East they say: 'The Mother is the first Guru, the Father is the second Guru, and the Guru is the third Guru.'

Two

NEW PLACES TO HIDE

Above: Dad's signing-on picture, 13th August 1940

The Germans moved us three times during the first year of the Blitz. We always managed to stay in Canal Road but by the time we took up residence in 104, Auntie Julie, my godmother, had married George Canham. As he was conscripted into the Army, she lived with us. Uncle Harry was in the Air Force and Aunt Maude was still in her teens. So apart from Grandad, I was the only male in the house. I should imagine I wasn't short of attention, and certainly, judging by early shots in the family album, I had a pretty snappy line in handknitted two-pieces. I used to go shopping in the street market with my gran but she never bought me any gear. It was my mother and my aunts who developed my sense of dress. Obviously, they didn't realise just what a rod for their backs they were making.

Life in East London during war-time was thrilling and full of incident if you were young. Most nights, even before the air raid warning sounded, I would have my favourite green siren suit put on over my pyjamas and be taken down into the shelter in the back yard. It had that sour odour of blankets which have been wet and never ever smell quite like dry ones again. It wasn't disagreeable; it was just a part of that underground magic with spluttering night lights, shadowy corners, stone hot water-bottles and cocoa. Outside, bangs and tremors, which just added to the excitement. Even on the occasions when we surfaced next day to find the house wrecked or too badly hit to return to, everybody just packed up as many belongings as could be salvaged and we all moved to the nearest empty house along the street. My pram came in handy on those mornings and I didn't use it much after my first birthday, when I just got up and walked straight to my grandad when he came home from work. Apparently my mother wanted me not to wear nappies – she worried about bandy-legs – so, having no husband to tend to and plenty of time, she just held me out after every feed and dressed me in knickers and then trousers. (Granny Stamp was speechless at my early training.)

Toys were extremely hard to come by in war-time, and the first toy I remember, besides Alf's homemade ones, was a red pedal car with yellow embellishments. This was obviously secured at great cost to the family, and was purchased to distract me from noticing that my Aunt Julie, to whom I'd become very attached, was away in hospital having her first child, a daughter christened Denise. I was two years old and my reign as only grandchild was about to end, but the ruse worked temporarily; I was so thrilled with the car that I even ate my lunch off the window-sill in the yard seated in it. This car travelled with me for years, as far as Chadwin Road. Its toy-town red and yellow rusted off and Dad painted it British racing green. However, I grew distant from Julie after Denny arrived. Not that she felt any less for me, I'm sure, because she has always been supportive of me, even at times when no one else was. It just shows the degree to which I demanded attention.

My Aunt Maude says that Julie was the one in our family with aspirations, and with Ethel out at work and Julie home pregnant, we spent a lot of time together and she may have infected me. Certainly later on, when I began to get outlandish ideas, Julie was the only one I felt comfortable sharing them with. Right up until I was eighteen, I would drop in on her whenever I felt the need to luxuriate in a proper bath.

There was a curious junction where Burdett Road joined Mile End Road. It was known as the Bohème Corner. Originally there had been a small narrow cinema, but it had been hit early in the Blitz and all that remained of it was the first row of seats and the

Above: Julie marries George Canham

Above left: Another day, another outfit

Above right: Me and Maude with Denise

front wall on to which the films had been projected. It was a surreal spot and to this day it hasn't been rebuilt although advertising hoardings dress the site and one can't see if the seats are still riveted to the concrete. It fascinated me when we lived in Bow and, although I wasn't allowed to cross the main Burdett Road on my own, I would often sit in one of the seats while my mum and I waited for the 106 bus to take us to Poplar, quite happy staring at the wall where the screen had been. I don't recall the first actual film that I was taken to, but the Bohème was my first cinema. I remember going with Mum to Commercial Road to have some photos done when we were caught in an air raid. We were hustled into the basement of Woolworth's at Aldgate: it was such a crush that Mum clasped me to her chest for a full hour. When the 'all clear' sounded and we returned to the street, she was so exhausted we sat on the doorstep of Bloom's and watched the fire engines arriving at Gardner's Corner. There's no mother like a tiger in the thick of adversity.

Every Christmas I was bought a new suit and, provided there was enough cash, I was fully kitted out. The Christmas before we were bombed out of Canal Road for the last time, I was three and a half. We went into every shop along Commercial Road. It was only at Gardner's Corner that I found a salt and pepper tweed number I liked! This choosiness extended even to the wine gums I was allowed to purchase by myself from Druce's corner shop. I was often given a penny to buy myself sweets, but every time my mother passed the shop after one of my forays, the shopowner would ask Ethel for a ha'penny.

'I'm sorry, dear, I always try to give him the cheap ones but he just won't have them. He just points to the Rowntree's and stares at me till I give them to him.'

I mention these incidents to give some idea of what Dad would have to contend with when the War finished and he returned to his young wife. Mum told me that before Dad went back to sea, he often took me out in the pram on his own 'as proud as anything'!

A lot of terrible things happened to Dad in the War. He was shipwrecked several times when his ship lost the convoy and they were attacked like sitting ducks with no guns, just loaded with produce. But two incidents stayed in my mind. One was told to me by my mother who'd heard it from Dad's shipmates on shore leave, and the other he told me himself during my 'flower power' years after I had introduced him to a little Lebanese Red. The first was when everyone on board received a cable informing them that 'London was on fire' and shortly afterwards Dad received a second wire. Without opening it, he tried to throw himself over the side, believing it contained news that we had been killed. It took four guys to stop him and hold him while the envelope was opened and Dad read the message, 'Wife and child evacuated to Colne, Yorkshire'. His mate told Ethel, 'He calmed down but he was as white as a sheet and didn't eat any breakfast.'

What had actually happened was that I was taken North by Mum during the heaviest bombardment of London. The journey to the small town on the Yorkshire–Lancashire border and my first train ride made deep impressions on me. I recall Kate instructing Mum to dress me in my siren suit for the trip: 'He'll need that up there, Et.' I did too; we arrived to the first snow I'd ever seen, and were welcomed into the saintly Mrs Watson's home as if we were her own kin. Being only two, I was often sat astride their large Alsatian for rides in the fields. The snow drifts were so deep that we often had to climb out of the front room windows to dig the snow away from the front door. I was sorry to leave the Watson household, and have always felt good with Northern folk, but Ethel missed her family and we stood in the corridor of the troop-filled train all the way South. Mrs Watson never failed to send Mum a Christmas greeting with a little of her hand-crochet work right up until she passed away a few years back.

The second event, which Tom told me himself, was during a winter run from England and up to Iceland when his ship ran into a Force 10. The captain decided to put the ship into the eye of the storm under full power. In the boiler room, up to their waists in Arctic water, with head and shoulders in a fiery inferno, Dad and the other donkey man shovelled coal into the ship's boiler for twelve hours, while the ship at full steam remained in the same place. Stokermen didn't even warrant a uniform in the Merchant Navy. Dad's only medal was his hair which was stone-grey the following day. At the end of this trip when he returned to us not a trace of his wonderful black hair remained.

Meanwhile the family, reckoning it would be tempting fate to move a fourth time into Canal Road, settled farther east in Plaistow. The name originally meant sportsground or play-place, but by the time we landed there all that remained of its village-green atmosphere was a cobbled triangle in front of the pub and cinema, both of which bore the name Greengate. Just past this Greengate was 603 Barking Road, E.13. It was a much bigger house, on the main road, with a cellar and a coal chute. The two front rooms were connected by double doors. Into the room overlooking Barking Road went the piano and overmantel, and the back housed a fold-out sofabed for the menfolk on leave. Ground-floor back was the main living-room, with coal stove and oven which Gran zebra'd black and shiny immediately. This room had a door into the scullery which opened on to a garden and outside loo.

But upstairs on the landing was a bathroom and a loo inside! They say a house whose numbers add up to nine is good for evolving and, although 603 was a wonderful house for children, revealing unexpected secrets and lots of places to hide, looking back it witnessed some profound sadnesses for the Perrott family. First, Alf was diagnosed as tubercular and taken to a sanatorium. He never returned to Barking Road except to be taken off by black horses. Maude had an unsuccessful marriage to a handsome Scorpio scallywag, another sailor. It lasted about five minutes, although I did get to wear a white satin suit and sit next to the driver in the big Daimler that took everyone to St Andrew's Church. Uncle Harry failed his pilot's medical because a piece of his eyelid was missing. He was so disappointed that he transferred to the Royal Navy, but he never really liked it. Finally, my shopping trips with Gran ended; she didn't take to the new neighbourhood and rarely left the house.

We hadn't been in Plaistow long before Mum got me embroiled with the local cub scout troupe. I had no sooner become accustomed to bowing down to the old wolf twice a week than we got wind of a cub and scout collective going off to camp in Dorset. Probably urged on by Kate, who didn't want to see her grandson left out of anything, I was packed off to a patch under canvas right near the sea at Corfe Castle. I've always found it odd that Mum sent me off so young. She wasn't the type to put her kids down for playschool before they were born and I certainly didn't make great demands on Kate's time, who'd weathered nine pregnancies and grabbed me whenever she could. I was content to sit in my pushchair as if stoned, just watching Kate do her housework. I think both my mum and dad were a bit naïve when they first married; probably some well-dressed woman in a queue told Ethel that sea air would put colour in my cheeks. It did that all right! In truth, the field chosen for this Akela excursion was an enchanting spot loaned to the scouts by a Colonel Scott and his wife Daphne on their estate in Kingston. But the fact is I can only appreciate it in retrospect, as most of the time I felt too homesick to get out of bed in the morning. Even when taken on the two-mile hike into Corfe itself, I kept the picture of Mum and Gran in my mind, breathing them in and out constantly like a sacred *mazifa*, and spent all my time in the village at a souvenir shop sorting out a present my pocket money would stretch to. I finally settled on a spoon for

Mum's tea caddy with Corfe enamelled on the handle. I can't explain the stress or the relief at seeing my mother waiting outside the church hall when the charabanc finally returned. I haven't been one for holidays since. I like to travel but preferably with a motive other than 'to have a good time'.

Ethel and I moved out to 124 Chadwin Road, near the public lido, after my brother Chris was born, and although there wasn't often a day when I didn't walk or trolleybus the length of Prince Regent's Lane over the hill to see my nan, life was never really the same for me after we left 603.

I just couldn't get by without her company, the marmalade sandwiches and Sunday high teas with winkles and celery purchased from the horse and cart that cruised the streets at weekends. She always arranged for me to get the stump which was my favourite part (whatever happened to celery stumps?). When Mum went into hospital on the night of 6 July '42, I was in bed and didn't notice her going. But years later she told me that when she came home she caught a 699 trolleybus from the hospital to the Greengate. From there it was just a stroll down Barking Road past Bates's Bike Shop to 603. Gran and I had come out to the front to see if she was coming.

'As I got near the house I saw you holding Nan's hand and waiting at the gate. You saw me coming and your face lit up. You moved towards me and then I saw you look at the bundle in my arms. Your face darkened and you put your head into Nan's side. My heart turned over.'

Sibling rivalry can be an intense emotion. They say the mind starts to form when the first teeth arrive, but is the individual ego already so strong so young? Sylvana Mangano told me that she was once in a car with her two-year-old daughter, Veronica, and just starting to show with her second, Raphaela. She saw Veronica looking at her stomach and suddenly the two year old was pounding the bulge in rage with little clenched fists.

My own ambivalent feelings towards my younger brother Chris were compounded by two events. The first thing was that I was made to go to school, which was to me like a huge rejection. I know that most mothers love to get their kids off to school, playgroups or nurseries the sooner the better, but I have really quizzed Ethel about this and it seems that she believed she would get into trouble if she didn't send me. She said it was painful for her as well as embarrassing, as I would hang on to the dreadful school railings and beg her not to make me go. One morning I was on my knees outside the school gates with my hands pressed together as if in prayer and tears in my eyes, saying, 'Please, Mummy, please don't send me, Mummy.'

Above and right: Two faces of sibling rivalry

As she passed us, a well-to-do woman commented, 'Whatever are you doing to that poor child? You must be wicked.'

Ethel, bright red in the face, dragged me off shopping with her to Rathbone Street Market. My brother, John, overhearing this tale of Ethel's one Sunday, said, 'Christ, Tel, were you always so over the top?'

Actually, Faraday or Holborn Road School was a nightmare. It was one of those red-brick Victorian Gothic monstrosities that could easily have doubled for an asylum in a Hammer Horror movie. It was no wonder that when I was pushed through the gates, it didn't take me long to work out that all I had to do was to get my name ticked off in the register, be excused for a pee just before the form teacher handed over to the next one, and slide back through the gates and into Beckton Road Park with its swings, slides, bandstand and bowling green, to say nothing of the open-air lido, which was full of interest in the summer if you could find a plank with a knot-hole knocked out. Of course, this couldn't go un-noticed indefinitely and Mum did get wind of it in the end. I was carted off to old Dr Brown who, bless his medical heart, advised Mum that perhaps four was just a little young and it would be perfectly all right to wait until I was five.

The loss of the family unit was another blow. In Canal Road I had grandparents and a whole bevy of aunts and uncles. The formulation changed but there was always this big cushion of human warmth, protecting me from the chill of the outside world. Subconsciously, I must have wanted this kingdom of childhood to stretch until I was no longer a child. Plenty of time for the limitations of adulthood when one is old enough to be aware of the confines of being an individual. As a child I had no sense of separation with anybody or anything. I don't use the word kingdom lightly. This wrench, the first tear in the fabric, came when Mum moved to Chadwin Road. I was usurped by a younger man, and, to compound my fears, I was compelled to go to school. How strange it is that every parent who suffers the pain of separation from his or her parents does exactly the same when entrusted with children of their own. It's not unlike circumcision really; they just can't wait to get the old knife in.

Waking up was the worst part. There was no friendly hiss of the gas light with the irregular popping of the mantel, the wonderful aroma of Gran lightly burning the toast. I can picture her small body exactly, standing in front of the stove with the two inside iron rings removed from the top and a slice of bread on a toasting fork thrust into the red circle, the heat of the fire on her hands, and giving an extra glow to her prominent cheekbones. As she grew older the skin just seemed to grow finer and tighter around her cheeks and forehead. She seemed impervious to heat, even topping up her cups of tea with boiling water from a kettle always at the ready. I tried to emulate her in everything, but I couldn't master this boiling tea trick. Years later I came across a dervish who downed his tea in the same manner to the delight and astonishment of his mureeds. 'It denotes great internal fire,' one said to me in awe. Well, I suppose Kate had that all right. If Gran took against neighbours, you had to be sorry for them, and I've seen Alf behave as though he wasn't with her when traders were getting the rough edge of her tongue. For me it was just great. This four-foot-ten-inch tall firework was like having a compact battleship all of my own, although she had a heart of wax under that tough exterior. The smallest compliment would bring a flush to her face and she would go to immense trouble to give pleasure. She always managed to hide away a few chestnuts at Christmas so that on New Year's Eve, which she and I always managed to spend together, staying up till midnight, out they would come from the back of the drawer. She would cut a corner off each and I would roast them on a shovel. We brought in twelve New Years like this, in front of the fire with the lights out, and the room still festive with the paper chains we made, sticking the colour strips together with flour and water. We never took our decorations down until Twelfth Cake Day, when we finished off the Christmas cake, or if it had gone already, Gran made another one using rice and wheat flour to get just the right crunch. I was having tea at the Mayfair Regency in New York recently and spied Pound Cake on the menu. As it was that time of year when the city is sprucing itself up to be Christian, and as I was indulging in a little nostalgia, I ordered a slice, but, even at $4.50, neither Gran nor I would have given it to Pieshop, my rabbit.

On one of Gran's rare trips outside her house to have a look at our new quarters, she came upon Mum trying to force my head through the neck of a pullover she'd knitted me and cast off too small. Not wanting to admit to herself that she'd done the work for nothing, she practically had my ears off, dragging the thing on to me. Nan took in my red face and said to Mum, 'If you don't always treat that boy proper, I'll come back and haunt you.' She was that protective of all her grandchildren.

Gran once bought me a ticket for a Whist Drive, sold to her by a hawker who came to the door. Neither she nor I had any idea what Whist was, let alone a Drive, and I still don't. But I duly turned up at a local school behind the Co-op, to find a smoke-filled hall packed with grown-ups sitting around tables playing cards in intent groups. As I was only eight, I beat an unnoticed exit but every time I even think about that Whist Drive, it brings tears to my eyes. Perhaps it's connected with Maria's Box, or rather its contents.

Maria, or Ria as she was called by the family, was Kate's mother, and as a young girl she had been put into service in a grand country house outside London. At a certain point the young man of the household, turned on by Ria's lustrous black curls, and no doubt feeling the attraction between social opposites, began trifling with her. Ria packed her box with her few possessions and left the house one night. It was while she was sitting on her box-trunk, waiting for the stage coach to take her back to London and the lying-in home, that Willmore happened by, and, being equally taken by the black ringlets that insisted on curling on to her forehead no matter how regularly they were scruffed back, accompanied her on the London stage coach and soon married her. They moved into the upstairs part of a house in Duckett Street.

William Willmore was an Irishman, skilled in the making of small arms and employed at the Proof House, a gunsmith's in Commercial Road, Aldgate. Ria's maiden name was Groom, and although there is no evidence of her first child, a girl, ever being registered she was known throughout her life as Julia Willmore. Ria had four more children and a good marriage. Catherine, my gran, was her youngest daughter and it was she who told me of her mother's box which was kept locked under the bed and no one was allowed to see inside it. Not until Emma, her last surviving child, died was the sombre secret in Ria's box discovered.

When Alfred Perrott married Catherine Willmore, his sister stopped speaking to him. Apparently she was disgusted by his 'marrying down'. The Perrotts were of French origin, supposedly of Huguenot blood. Alf did speak French and read Latin. He was known as 'the aristocrat' around Canal Road, mainly due to his bearing and reserved manner. All his kids passed their exams to go

New Places to Hide

Above: My Great-Grandmother Ria

to the high school, but he allowed none of them to attend. My Auntie Julie says he would not risk them looking down on their mother once they became educated. My Aunt Maude thinks he didn't want the extra expense and encouraged them to attend night school once they were paying their own way.

While we were in Bow, it was customary to live part of the time on the street. Whether this was due to the minute proportions of the interiors or to delay turning on the gas light and putting the pennies in the meter, it was a part of a social fabric which allowed most front doors to remain ajar. A street like Canal Road was really a big living-room. Certainly during the Blitz it was perfectly all right to nip into any neighbour's house if caught short by a warning siren. On most summer and autumn evenings, out would come a chair on to the pavement, accompanied by knitting or crochet and a little social interchange. It was probably such characteristics of East End life which gave the Cockney a strong sense of 'surround', and a unity to draw from. I know there is an awful lot of bullshit about the 'chirpy' London working class, but there is a certain saltiness or, as my friend Terence Donovan says, 'steeliness' that is instantly discernible no matter how far from home. This is probably what Donovan meant when he told another great chum of mine, Nickolas Grace, 'Don't believe all that guff about Stamp being a Cockney. He was brought up in Plaistow, and that's like chalk and cheese.'

The move farther east from Bow did ensure us more physical safety but it brought us into an area that was populated with a breed of people I'd not encountered before: the middle class. In E.13 these genteel inhabitants were invaded by the hordes getting away from the terrible pounding of central London and the dockland. Here we were exposed to a life-style that wasn't unattainable, like the squires of Tredegar Square, but near and similar enough to allow us to think we were entitled.

I began to experience envy, and a terrible dissatisfaction with my lot. In fantasy this took the form of imagining an elegant woman arriving outside our house in a black limousine and claiming me as her lost heir. I would be whisked off, my rightful dukedom restored to me. I would wear a suede waistcoat and effect a monocle. Or 'down hopping' (picking hops in Kent), I would come across the spoilt daughter of some local landowner, who looked remarkably like Jean Simmons. She would fall for me in some unthought-out

New Places to Hide

Above: Uncle Harry

circumstances and her father would be forced to bestow on me property and riches as befitted a mate to his loved one. I'd acquire a horse, riding breeches, silk shirts with cavalier sleeves, and we'd go riding together. The harshness of reality merely increased as I got older. My mother would not let me wear jerseys and boots like the other kids on the street, so while I attended Faraday School I was ostracised for being above myself. I don't remember having any friends my own age although I did naturally strike up acquaintances with elderly people and I still do.

After I suffered the first year at school, a small miracle happened. The grading of the terrible Faraday was changed. It became Holborn Road Secondary Modern for eleven year olds who failed the eleven-plus. The minor inmates were split into two groups and those of us who resided to the east of the school were transferred to Tolgate Primary School. This meant a slightly longer walk so I had to leave home earlier, but you could cut across the Rec., jumping the ditch which bounded one side and slice a few minutes off the journey, giving time for an extra cup of tea and another slice of toast if Mum was in the mood. The school building, nowhere near as old as Faraday, was on only two floors. Pupils started on the ground floor at the back looking out over the playing field, and graduated year by year to the second-floor front where, aged ten and eleven, hopefully we were ready to pass the scholarship.

Life improved. We no longer had to pass the horse slaughter-house between Brown's sweet shop and Faraday – it was a gruesome irony that the location of this abattoir, with its stench, glimpses of men in yellow rubber covered in blood, and the tragic whinnying of the horses who knew full well what was about to happen, was directly opposite St Cedd's Church, the local Anglo-Catholic place of worship, making the Brock and Chadwin Road corner a hive of activity what with one thing and another. Mother hadn't yet leaned on me to join the choir, and Brown's had long since run out of stock and never had a single sweet until after the War, no matter how many ration coupons you had, so I abandoned that end of the street. For the first few years at Tolgate, learning by rote wasn't too seriously enforced. We had random 'intelligence tests' when we were all herded into the top assembly hall and papers were given out which we had to complete in pencil, answering questions like: 'Draw the letter E as seen in the mirror'.

Above: St Cedd's choir

I suppose I was OK with this stuff because I was promoted to the 'A' form in my second year. Mr Smith, a good-looking man with a Ronald Colman moustache, took art classes. He always started lessons by doing a spectacular drawing on the blackboard, so we were all suckers for him and I learned to be not at all bad at art.

Mum was an avid movie goer, so whenever she had an extra bob or so, she would take me to the pictures. Gary Cooper in *Beau Geste* at the old Grand has left such a strong impression on me that it may well have been the first movie I went to. Uncle Harry often took me to the cinema, and I remember one glorious outing when we sat in the front row of the circle at the Boleyn Odeon and saw *The Razor's Edge*, with Gene Tierney and Tyrone Power – wow! He bought me a whole box of Pontefract cakes which made it just about perfect. The main film was preceded by the Pathé-News, which always showed footage of the War. I recall asking Mum what they showed when there wasn't a war. In '45 the War finished and Dad came home. I ate my first banana.

Three

MUM PASSES ME THE BARAKA

Above: Two Tigers

Mum Passes Me the Baraka

V.E. Day was euphoric – the street parties, house fronts and gardens all decorated, and the gaiety at 603 to celebrate the homecomings of Harry, Uncle George, Julie's husband and Dad unscathed, with the connecting doors of the front rooms thrown open, Mum playing 'Knees Up, Mother Brown' on the piano, booze all over the place and everyone sleeping everywhere. I had never been at such joyous family gatherings. I was only sad that Alf wasn't there to enjoy it with us. He had died the year before and had lain in his coffin in the same room where they were now threatening to tear Mrs Brown's legs right off. I'd been held up to have a last look at my grandad. How cold his face was when I kissed him. The following day the hearse with the black-plumed horses took him to be buried and we followed slowly in the same kind of black cars that had taken us to the wedding. Mum let me choose the flowers, and I watched them being thrown into the hole after they lowered Alf's coffin. The horse-drawn hearse carrying Grandad's body to its final resting place was the last I saw in England. Nan said he was in a better place and I thought it was a wonderful way to go, and fitting for him. Alfred Perrott was an aristocrat in the real sense of the word.

It was tough on my dad, coming home after the War. He was still a young man, of course, but with his prematurely grey hair he must have felt his youth was gone. I remember how upset he was one Bank Holiday at a fair on Hampstead Heath, where some charlatan guessed my parents' ages; Mum twenty-eight, Dad fifty-two. Seeing how white Tom went, the guy apologised.

'Much grey,' he said, touching his hair.

Tom must also have felt a bit like an intruder returning to a house where I had become a substitute object of Ethel's passion. I didn't take too kindly to a rival. He was also ill, psychologically ill, although nobody knew that at the time. Tom was convinced that he had something growing in his head, and the pain took him to doctors and hospitals for months, until he wound up with a bright psychiatrist at the Seaman's Hospital in Stepney.

The doctor talked to him at length, assured him there was nothing growing in his head, and explained that, as a result of living for so long under such dangerous conditions, his brain had been forced to adapt to it and now, with the stress suddenly lifted, his mind could not adjust to the new situation. Tom left the hospital and strolled down Commercial Road intending to stop by Mills

Grove and buy his mother a drink. He was drawn into the barber shop which used to be opposite the entrance to the Blackwall Tunnel. He ordered the works, trim, singe and shave. He was the only customer. The old barber unhurriedly went to work on him, rhythmically snipping away at his still luxuriant head of hair, carefully singeing the ends with a wax taper which filled the shop with that pleasant acrid aroma. After briskly rubbing his hair with Dad's favourite, Bay Rum, he angled back the chair and draped the hot towels over Tom's face. Tom felt himself relaxing more and more. As he touched different parts of his body with his awareness it seemed just to melt away. His brain emptied itself as though a big snowball was rolling around inside his head and gathering up the stray thoughts. His whole body just slipped away. He was safely in the reclining chair, the hot towels in contact with his skin, but at the same time he felt lifted up out of himself, suspended in the air above his body. It seemed as though he stayed like that for hours. The sensation continued when the barber stropped his open razor and the leathery sound reached into Tom's orbit. The feeling remained as the shave started and progressed with incredible gentleness. Dad told me, 'I wanted to just be there for ever.'

Above: Chadwin Road V.E. party

Mum Passes Me the Baraka

When he stepped out into the street he knew he was cured.

The conflict, or lack of empathy, between Dad and me was not immediately apparent. I was too taken up with trying to keep Mum's attention. But later, when I sought Dad's affection, I found he was almost indifferent to me. Chris and I were never real mates, partly because of sibling rivalry and partly probably because Dad, observing me as a 'cissy' product of a solely feminine household (what with my rarefied interest in clothes and finicky appetite, he had enough cause), decided to bring Chris up himself, or at least to influence him. I soon had to stop fighting with my younger brother because it was just too dangerous. Dad taught Chris how to look after himself and he quickly became very husky. Although our bone structure was almost identical, he, unlike me, didn't pick at his food. He just ate everything, my leavings included. Even Tom got into the habit of saying, 'Give it to the gannet.' Chris grew much weightier than me and stayed heavy until he worked with Leslie Caron, had a crush on her and ate only apples for three months.

People who know both my brother Chris and me often ask what it was like at home when we all lived there. The fact is that Richard, Chris and I were born at four-yearly intervals. Add to this that we are completely differing archetypes, each inheriting varying characteristics of our parents, which made our life within the confines of 124 rather structured to say the least. If you imagine a fearless scientist, a swash-buckling adventurer and a stroller-player layabout awash on a raft, you wouldn't be far out. A friend of mine says the trouble with family is that you don't get to choose them. Looking at my sibs from this point of view, I consider that I didn't do at all badly. We are all our own people and this perhaps saved us from becoming an ingrown household. It never occurred to me to try to influence any of them. If I had to hit the nail on the head with a short description, I'd say we were austere without being harsh towards each other. In the Sixties, when I started taking chums home to 124 for the Sunday lunch, one girlfriend remarked, 'God, you Stamps are frightening, you're so polite to each other.'

Chris was a natural fighter, but a street fighter. He hated any kind of formal training and, when entered for the school boxing championships, he received byes until the quarter-finals which were held in the town hall where he was soundly beaten by a lanky skinny kid who had silk shorts and proper boxing boots. Chris's response was to wait outside the hall until his opponent came out

Above: Rare picture of Tom and his three sons

and knock him senseless. Chris enjoyed a fight – a trait which held him in good stead during his rock and roll years later. I, on the other hand, was so fearful of getting beaten up that if cornered I just went for any available jugular to finish the danger immediately. This was soon recognised at Tolgate after I was picked on by one of the fearsome Madel twins. Luckily, there was a master on hand, who discovered me with my hands around poor twinnie's neck and banging the back of his head against a coat hook in the downstairs cloakroom. Chris was also a Cancerian like Dad and me (an awful lot of crablike sidewalking went on inside the thin walls of Chadwin Road), but unlike me his ascendant was in Leo. In that sense he was an equal measure of Ethel and Tom. Of course, we didn't know much about that kind of stuff but, when I finally learned to read, I enjoyed Gypsy Petulengro in Mum's *Woman's Own*, in which 22 July was the first day of Leo, and not the last day of Cancer, making me believe myself to be a lion like Mum, not a crab like Tom and Chris.

Mum Passes Me the Baraka

There was always a callous element in Dad's attitude to me, and although I was only belted by him once – surprisingly at Ethel's insistence – from very early on it was evident. There is a story in the Stamp folklore of us on a Sunday afternoon visit to Nanny Stamp. I was all of one and a half. It seems my eye fell on what I took to be a bowl of custard in the middle of her dining table and I started to climb up to get it. Mum tried to stop me, recognising the particularly strong concoction (Colman's mustard powder and vinegar) used in the Poplar household. Dad restrained her by saying, 'Let him find out for himself.'

Reaching my target, I filled a handful, a mouthful, and quickly learnt my lesson.

I actually remember him smoking a cigarette and, seeing how it fascinated me, offering to show me how he could blow smoke out of his ears. 'Just put your hand here,' indicating his stomach, 'and watch my ears.' He inhaled deeply and, while I attentively obeyed, he touched my hand with the lighted end of his fag.

It must have been a terrific struggle for Tom and Ethel to provide us with the bare necessities, let alone the extra 'stuff' a lot of the other kids seemed to have. I remember pestering them for my first football boots and then for a cricket bat. They provided the boots but a bat was outside their budget. Dad got a lump of willow from somewhere and hand-carved a bat out of it. It was an odd shape, rather narrow, and being a solid piece it was heavy and clumsy. I didn't really appreciate it. It was another reminder of how much poorer we were than other families. To commemorate the occasion Dad took my mate, Johnny Tanner, and myself over to Beckton Park where seven winds met, seven winds! He drew a chalk wicket on one of the big plane trees and put Johnny in to bat. He hit our bowling all over the place, with me running for what seemed like hours before we got him out. I went into bat and Tom bowled me out first ball. I wouldn't have it. He insisted. I threw down the bat and sulked off home. Looking back over my shoulder, I saw Dad continuing to bowl to Johnny. It was the only time he had played with me and I had blown it. It must have been a real disappointment to Dad. I was ashamed of myself for weeks but of course I wouldn't own up to it.

Shortly after that, when I was about nine, Mum enrolled me at Fairbairn and Mansfield House Boys' Club. I always assumed that it was her idea but recently she told me, 'No, your dad found out about it. It was his idea to take you. He knew they did boxing there and wanted you to start. Make a man of you, he thought. I was worried about your looks and didn't want you to get hurt, but he said that's the way he should learn, so he knows how to take care of himself.'

Fairbairn House was so grand I couldn't believe it. I was even more amazed that I hadn't noticed the building before. It was in the main Barking Road, practically opposite the old Grand cinema, between the Abbey Arms pub, where Mum worked as a barmaid, and Leaches clothes shop, where she bought us Christmas suits with her 'club money'. But I had taken up with a gang of kids none of whom would have been much interested in a boys' club whose glass-plated doors were engraved with boxing gloves, snooker balls, table-tennis bats and masks of drama; they were too preoccupied with territorial stone fights with the Hudson gang on the nearby debris of Egham and Chalk Road.

Johnny Straffon lived in the house whose garden backed on to the side of ours. The two houses were separated by a bigger building occupying the corner of Chadwin and Egham: the Hobbses' house. Johnny had ginger hair, which came in handy when the 'William' books became the rage; he was a natural for William's lieutenant, Ginger. Next door to the Straffons were the Clearys who had lots of kids, although only the sulky Violet was our age, and then the Pearsons, whose son Tommy, our occasional gang leader, was a maverick and only deigned to lead us when it suited him. Tall and gaunt with that narrow rib-cage and flat chest associated with a Samurai caste, he was hard to contain in hand to hand, and with a catapult would have rivalled David himself, able at any time to hit half a stale loaf at fifty feet firing between his legs. Next to his house was 'our' debris, three or four houses wide and as deep as the Pearson house and garden. It was not even bomb damage, just a space left when the Council ran out of cash. Opposite our territory was a magnificent wasteland, running along the whole of the top end of Egham Road from the Beckton main road to Chalk Road, with odd-shaped urban ruins and two huge old trees. My first sexual encounter happened in the branches of the bigger of these sentinels but it was pre-erection and I'm ashamed to say that other than its being warm and definitely homosexual I don't remember anything else about it.

This wasteland stretched across about two hundred yards and

finished directly on the back yards of Salomons Road where the infamous Hudsons lived, a set of ferocious brothers and sisters, including identical twins, two boys a year younger than myself, who, because of their physical similarity and fighting power which totalled more than the sum of the ingredients, were endowed with all kinds of mythical attributes. I was a little in awe of the twins, who reminded me of the foxes in my Rupert Bear annuals, and often dreamed what fun it must be to be two. I could never quite follow my mother's superstitious caution, 'Don't do that or one of us will have ginger twins,' whenever I finished making a pot of tea she had started. The Hudson gang mostly stayed near the eastern side of the debris, and we shared with them the remaining two-thirds alternately, although there was no laid-down arrangement. There weren't 'no-go' areas in the streets and in fact the actual eruptions were probably as much lunar as anything else. There were regular stone fights and I was hit twice, once on my left cheekbone, and more seriously when a brick landed an inch to the left of my eye and not much above my temple, hard enough for Douglas Rankin, when casting a Player's cigarette commercial, to remark, 'Yeah, he's interesting looking but too scarred for our product.' Apparently, the same day this doyen of screen advertising said of the unknown Jean Shrimpton, 'Get that horse outa here.'

The cuts on my face probably started my mother thinking of ways to get me out of the neighbourhood gang. She was single-minded about how I appeared to the world and she imprinted on me a belief that I was destined for a better life than ours was then, when Dad never brought home more than £12 a week and always had to work like a dog whatever employ he was in. As our family grew, Christopher Thomas in '42, Richard Francis in '46, Mum arranged to work an evening shift as a barmaid, alternating between the Iron Bridge Tavern in Canning Town and the Abbey Arms at the top end of New Barn Street. Dad never really approved but I'm sure she enjoyed these nocturnal outings, and as a provider of drinks she was the centre of attraction, after a fashion. I would watch her getting ready to go to work, powdering her face and rolling her bottom lip over the top one the way women do when they apply lipstick, and lastly a dab of California Poppy or Nuit de Paris behind the ears, which I knew to be the final touch in this protective but come-hither coating.

I always felt sad when she left the house. Loneliness out of all proportion to the fact, as though she would never return. The living-room seemed large, dim and threatening. My presence didn't fill the space; she took her light with her. When I lived with a geisha in Kyoto, on the first morning I left the house she waved me goodbye and began to cry. When I returned I questioned her about it. 'One moment, one chance. When you go I feel you go for ever because in truth life is this moment. We geisha do not assume any continuation.' That was how I felt when Ethel took off in the evening. I would scamper close to the fire, if there was one, or to the wireless. Anything to ease this feeling of life without her. On the occasions I have been badly let down by women, I have taken solace from a real fire and have always tried to live in places with proper fireplaces. One of the few jobs I did willingly at home was tending the fire; I lit it in the morning using only one match, and figured out how to make it work, even with sparse kindling. When they replaced the whole side of 124 and completely screwed up the chimney, I could always get it going without too much smoke if I had a newspaper big enough to create a good draught. I greatly loved lying in front of the fire, especially during puberty, when Dad took to calling me the 'horizontal champ'. Dad had nicknames for all of us; Chris was the 'ragged-trouser brigade' at that time, and Richard, whose complexion was darker than ours, was christened Omo.

I was not a person who particularly felt the cold – I dread central heating, and air conditioning gives me the creeps – but as a child I liked to absorb the fire heat right into me. I would watch the flames for hours. Mum went along with most of my oddities, feeling, I think, that she had set me on course. Having encouraged me to think of myself as special, she wanted to see what I would make of myself. But I remember how crushed she was after my having sat still for a whole term while some idiot of a teacher drivelled on through an alphabet of careers without covering any that remotely interested me. He answered my end-of-term enquiry about my own future with the words, 'You would make a good manager of Woolworth's.'

Ethel's face went white when I told her. She wasn't yet confident enough to question that kind of authority but it was obvious that she envisaged something different for her eldest, although she didn't know what. I recall a conversation about what we'd be if given a free choice, and she said, 'I'd like to be something there is only one of . . . like a Pope.'

When I played a Pope in a movie called *Death in the Vatican* it did cross my mind that perhaps I was acting out Ethel's fantasy, albeit only for a month.

Looking back, much of my life has been spent fulfilling my mother's expectations, and I don't feel resentful in any way. It is just that I wanted success as much for her as I did for myself, and at a certain point I had to defy her in order to go where I knew I could best fulfil her dreams as well as my own compulsions. But the dividing line is hazy, and all I can say for certain is that one way and another she was a helluva booster rocket! Or, as they say in astrological circles, a Leo mother has the power of love or the love of power.

In the world of esoterica, there is a term 'handing on the Baraka'. The Baraka is usually thought of as an object, sometimes a short stick made of scented wood or even a carved piece of ivory. It is symbolic, of course, but as it is something that is often given by the Guru to his successor – his Chela or pupil – it is wrongly invested with power in itself. I've even seen exotics embarking on the highly lucrative US Guru circuit, carrying this staff under their arm like a drill sergeant, as proof of enlightenment. I believe my mother handed me some inner power, or Baraka, shortly before my tenth birthday, which is traditionally when a Brahmin parent teaches his child to master the breath. (I didn't learn how to breathe until I was thirty-three, but that's another story.) I don't know if it was even conscious on Ethel's part, but it happened like this. First of all I have to confess that as a child I was timid, shy and very self-conscious, although within the family I was considered to have an old head on young shoulders. This confidence or air of certainty disappeared outside the familial circle, where I became a shivering lump the moment attention was focused on me, whether entering a room of strangers or being asked a question in class. So, when our last term at Tolgate Primary started, and Mr Eric Newby gave us our last assignment in English, I was reduced to a state of mental paralysis. The idea of choosing a piece of poetry (it seemed I had only mastered reading last term), committing it to memory and then being prepared to get up when called, go to the front of the class and recite it in front of everybody, friends and enemies alike, simultaneously pushed all three trauma buttons in young Terence

H. I was so frightened that I couldn't even get to the first hurdle, let alone jump it. I was so terrified it was as much as I could do to open the book of verse.

English was the last period every Friday. Normally Friday afternoon was the only one looked forward to, with a double period of art, a break, a story and a weekend of freedom, but now this thirty-five minutes of misery crouched at the end of the week, like some dark monstrosity. Every lesson I sat stiff, promising God that if I got through this time without being called I would choose a poem and learn it the next day. But then I put it out of my mind until the next torturous Friday rolled around. In some miraculous sort of way I didn't get called, but every time some dummy stumbled through an inane verse (a dummy smarter than me), and Mr Newby's eyes fell on to the pink paper of the class register in front of him, my heart was in my mouth. A fortnight to go until the end of term. The full turn of the screw. On the Monday (a day for learning) I was so freaked that I couldn't eat. I missed breakfast and, when I came home at lunch-time and smelt my favourite egg and chips being cooked in the scullery and spied on the draining board a structured bread and butter pudding all set to go in the oven, I didn't really know how to tell Mum I couldn't get anything down. I lounged in the doorway, not taking the step down into the little room where she was busy over the stove. The tawdriness of the brick boiler, the one brass cold-water tap without the rubber nozzle that everybody else seemed to have, didn't nag at me today. My brain had swelled and was stuck against the inside of my skull like semolina.

'What's the matter with you?'

I looked down at my new black Oxfords, bought too big so that I could grow into them, scuffed already.

'Nuffin'.'

'What?'

'There ain't nuffin' wrong.'

'Well, if there ain't nothing, there must be something, mustn't there?'

She could sound just like Zeno at times. I had never been able to fathom this smug conundrum of my mother's. Today I didn't have the energy to argue. I was on the point of tears. I headed over towards the open window by the sink. On the floor was our bucket with a large loaf floating in it (one of Mum's alchemies for resuscitating stale bread; later to be drained and rebaked in a number 8 oven). There were two pot-menders clenched to the bottom of the pail; they ogled up at me through the water one each side of the swollen loaf like a boss-eyed fish. I cracked. It all came out in a breathless torrent. My mother stared at me, her face a picture of incomprehension, which rapidly changed to absolute disbelief. I ran out of puff. We looked at each other. The spluttering of the chips was the only sound. I remember it as if it were yesterday. She considered, mentally assuring herself she had heard aright.

'You mean . . .'

She caught my eye, making certain I was listening.

'You mean a poem. You've got to learn a poem and say it in front of the whole class. Just you, on your own, with everybody watching?'

'Yes.'

'Well, that's wonderful. What's the problem?'

Nerves again, fingers in mouth, biting what little nails are left. How many times I'd tried to stop!

'Can't do it. Can't choose one. Can't learn . . .'

'Can't?' Snap of Leonine jaws. Eyes harden. 'Where's the book?'

'Book?'

'Where's the poetry book?'

I draw the book, like some poisonous talisman I can't let go of, from my pocket.

'Right.'

She grabs it. Turns off flame under the chips. 'Right.' Flicks through the book. Stops. Puts her foreshortened finger, the index on the left hand, crushed in a mangle doing the wringing as a girl, into the middle of the children's book of verse.

'This one, yes, we'll do this one.'

'Wha'?'

'Shut up. Stand over there.'

She pushes me against the door which leads out into the yard. The yard with the zinc bath hanging on the wall, brought in on Friday nights, bath night. The inside of the wooden door is painted battleship-grey, Dad's favourite colour.

'Now this is the first line, repeat it after me.'

She paused, made sure I was listening.

'"The Wooden Horse of Troy", by G. K. Chesterton.'

Every lunch-time before lunch we'd work on the poem. I got to know that kitchen door well.

The Friday dawned. During lunch-break we had what was to be our last practice. Towards the end of the lesson, just when I thought I had been overlooked once more, Mr Newby looked up and at me. 'Stamp,' he said.

I stood, walked to the front of the class and past his desk to a spot halfway between where he was sitting and the classroom door. I turned and faced the class. I waited a moment. The classroom suddenly felt hot. I took a deep breath. '"The Wooden Horse of Troy", by G. K. Chesterton.'

I paused, just to make sure everybody was listening. I looked out over the desks. I took another deep breath and launched myself into it. I used the same pace we'd rehearsed, the same intonation, even to nervously clearing my throat – as the great horse was pulled through the gates of the walled city and tension was building inside the wooden gift. At the end there was a silence. It went on for some time.

'Stamp,' said Mr Newby, 'that was marvellous. I think that's the best spoken poem I've heard at this school. Well done, well done, lad. I am going to give you ten out of ten.'

He clapped me on the back. I flushed and returned to my seat. I ran home from school, along Holborn Road under the cherry trees that never gave proper fruit, left into the posh end of Egham Road and finally I was knocking at 124, glaring through the coloured paper that Mum had stuck to the windows of the door to make them look like stained glass. She couldn't not be in. No, the living-room door opened and then the front door.

'I did it, I did it, just like you said.'

'And?'

'Ten out of ten. He marked me ten out of ten. Said it was the best he'd heard at Tolgate.'

'So he should,' she said.

She made little of it, but she had tea ready and my second favourite jam, strawberry, on the table in no time. Richard was asleep in his pram. We sat and had tea together, just the two of us. I could feel she was really pleased.

Looking back at that moment, I can see that my mother had given over to me all the dreams and longings she had for herself. Probably seeing what she'd settled for and realising she would never accomplish her ambitions, she had entrusted them to me, and sitting opposite me in our draughty living-room with its cock-eyed lino-covered floor that sloped towards the fireplace, my mother appraised me proudly but perhaps wondering if she had done the right thing. And for me there seemed to be born the most intense longing to show her that I wouldn't let her down, that somehow I would lift us all out of this squalor.

Four

ELEVEN-PLUS?

Above: Aunt Maude, seventh child of a seventh child

The first big opportunity was about to come. It was called the eleven-plus, or scholarship. If passed, a choice of grammar schools lay open. If not passed, a sentence at Faraday Secondary Modern, followed by a lifetime of hard labour, or that was how it was put to me as part of the emotional blackmail used to make sure I would pass, or at least that I would seriously try. Mum had passed her eleven-plus but her father, who hadn't believed in higher education with him footing the bill, had stopped her dream of going to Rains High School. 'You can go to night school when you're paying your own way.' She became a typewriter mechanic, met Dad, and that was more or less that. It was one of her dreams I inherited, along with the rest of the family – she must have been waiting to see if this generation, of which I was the first, would move into another octave. And, of course, I would get to wear a uniform. The family would see to it that I got a leather satchel bought with various endowment monies due. There might even be a bicycle in it. Every extra embellishment was an added weight on me. I fully realised the implications. This was the first big turn in the road. I wanted to go to the grammar school where the girls played netball in navy-blue gym slips. I had watched them for hours through the wooden palings opposite the fire station, and the boys, in long grey trousers, looked enviably mature and indifferent. I didn't want to sweep the playground at Faraday and become one of the hapless ones who went off to work at Ford's in Dagenham or drove a lorry at Tate & Lyle's in Silvertown. But how to do it? I just wasn't that good. School had always seemed a terrible imposition and I just hadn't been able to get behind it, so I had stopped trying. It had taken me a whole year to knit a bloody face flannel, which was black by the time Miss Miller took pity on me and finished it herself. I was really flummoxed. I descended into superstition, imagining that if I didn't step on any cracks in the pavement for a whole block, everything would be all right. One day at morning assembly, the rest of the school was dismissed after the song and announcements and the top year were invited to sit on the parquet wooden floor for a talk. It was a pep talk about the forthcoming test, or scholarship. It was explained that we would only be able to leave the set classroom between papers, so to make sure we'd emptied our bladders, and please bring a sharp pencil with us to complete the tests with. At the end of this short lecture, the ones who wanted to pass were asked to raise their hands. Naturally nobody did. It was considered really cissy to want to be one of the p.i.g.s who wore a uniform and went to Plaistow Grammar School. I had the awful feeling that if I didn't raise my arm and be counted, I would fail. I slowly put up my hand. The headmaster took it in.

'Yes, Stamp isn't it? Let's hope it is still up when the results come through.'

I spent the next days sharpening pencils. I must have had a dozen in my top pocket come the fateful morning. Walking to school that day across the Rec. and jumping the ditch, I had that sensation of seeing everything for the first time and almost simultaneously thinking it will never be the same as this again. When I come home today it will be over, done, changed irrevocably.

During the actual examination my mind was calm. When I realised time was a factor and we had to finish as much as we could, I decided I would not go back over anything but would just plough on and try to finish. Maths was first. It had always been a nightmare. The only term I had done well was when I sat next to Maureen Smith and she had let me copy hers. I was on my own today. I looked across at my mate, David Taylor. He looked relaxed enough, but his mum had her own flour-carrying business, and intended to send him to Pitman's, a private school. If only we had two cream-coloured lorries. English was next. My head seemed full of things to write about, and I wrote a composition as if I was writing a letter home from camp in Dorset with the Cubs. I'd been really homesick. The final paper was a general knowledge type of thing and I was relieved to discover that it wasn't unlike the intelligence tests we'd sat for. I fairly romped through that, without breaking a single pencil.

Well, it was over. I finished at Tolgate. Mr Newby gave me a rather old-fashioned look as I was saying goodbye. 'I don't know about you, Stamp,' he said. 'You're a monkey puzzle.'

I didn't know what he meant, so I asked Mum.

'It's a tree,' she said. 'I suppose he doesn't understand you. I don't think it's a nice thing to say.'

I was in limbo. The weeks went by. It was the slowest summer break I remember, and then the letter arrived from the West Ham County Education Committee. I had passed. Inside was a choice of schools. Please to fill in a second choice as first might not be available. God, we were excited. I couldn't believe I'd done it.

Mum got Richard ready and we walked round to Barking Road to tell Nan. She was as pleased as Punch and, although she didn't cry, her eyes watered a lot and she kept wiping them with a hanky she kept in her sleeve. She was very fierce about my having a proper outfit, 'As good as everyone else's,' and pocket money, 'If you don't give it, they'll find other ways of getting it,' and agreed with Mum and me that we should opt for Plaistow Grammar as it was halfway to her and I could come there and do my homework, where it was quiet. So Plaistow County Grammar School it was, with Stratford Grammar second, which would entail going to school on a bus. I remember going to Gran's front room which was always kept beautiful when she was alive. I just sat there in a kind of hush; the room always had an aroma like old books. I looked at the picture of Little Lady Bountiful giving food to the gypsies and took stock of how good I felt. Little did I know my life would become a series of intense efforts followed by long periods of almost non-activity. I would need to learn all there was to know about pressure and how to use it. In fact, in many ways I was to inherit my dad's ability to build up a head of steam and maintain it without blowing the boiler, but the boiler, in my case, was me. I was the machine which had to be kept steady and ready. I didn't always succeed.

Dad had been having a really hard time since the War. Jobs were scarce, and only the most menial were available to an unskilled sailor. He could turn his hand to anything, but he was a self-effacing man, and I don't think he knew how to push himself. I believe he considered it selfish to expect anything of anybody. He finally got a steady number at Cape Asbestos, and everything was going OK at home, when we were invaded by the insurance man. Mum always believed in insurance, or rather was frightened into taking policies we couldn't afford by the smooth operators who called with our endowment payments and didn't leave until we'd signed it all away again with new, even better policies which would bring us even more money, but not now. Except for this one time, Tom and Ethel had been sold a new Jerusalem. The salesman had whipped the new formula from his briefcase and was filling it in for them with his Conway Stewart pen. I was into fountain pens at the time and hoping for one at Christmas. Anyway, he asked Tom where his place of employ was (place of employ!) and Dad said he was employed regularly at the Cape.

'The Cape, Tom, I may call you Tom?'

Dad had hardly mouthed the word asbestos when the new panacea, which would make our life so easy, disappeared like greased lightning into the cone from which it had manifested itself in so lively a manner, and oh so jolly had his bowler on and was out of the door before you could say knife. Dad gave his notice in the next day. He didn't know what was wrong but he'd seen men running away from the dust chute and had asked his foreman why.

'Oh, it's nothing, son; if you're worried I'll arrange for you to get extra milk.'

To wash it down?

Asbestosis was unheard of in those days, but Dad figured if old crafty artful left without taking our money, he must have known something we didn't. He was right; Julie's husband and Tom's boyhood friend, George Canham, died of it and it was only because Julie wouldn't let it go, and took Cape to every court that would listen, that she became the first person to win a claim. £10,000. It didn't bring George back and it can't cure her own condition which was brought about through her washing his contaminated overalls. Cape maintained that the condition could be caused by smoking, but Julie wasn't a smoker so they gave her a few grand too. That was thirty-five years after the man from the Pru legged it from our two up, two down. Still, he did us a flavour, as the young Maurice Micklewhite used to say, because when Dad left Cape he got a job at the Union Lighterage Tug Company, and although he was back to stoking, he really only felt at home when somehow connected with water. He must have realised that the tidal hours, twenty-four on, twenty-four off, would suit his marriage as well as his nature. I'm sure my dad was a natural solitary, although everybody thought the world of him, and he always seemed to make everyone laugh. It became clear to me later in life that he, like myself, needed both. Like breathing in and out. My mother never completely understood this side of his character. Being on his own, she felt, was getting away from her. His stoicism in response to her emotional demands inflamed her further, and all of us witnessed their fights. Fight is the wrong word really, for Dad never retaliated physically. Even one Sunday when she grabbed a colander of boiling greens from the stove and threw the contents on to his bare chest, he just gasped 'God bloody blimey!', put on a jacket, took something from the cupboard under the stairs and left the house. Ethel ordered me to follow him.

'Don't let him out of your sight.'

'Why, Mum?' says I, not relishing having to follow Dad all afternoon.

'He's taken his cut-throat. He keeps it in there. You just stay with him.'

Of course, I couldn't keep with him. Once Dad realised I was monitoring his movements, he just charmed me into going back home. He said something like, 'She's a difficult woman to live with, boy. You'll understand when you grow up. You just go back home now.'

He always came back, but then he understood about pressure, and I wouldn't have put it past him to have taken his razor either to shave with if he stayed at the Seaman's Hostel – he was always clean-shaven – or, more likely, considering Ethel's reaction, to provoke just that. By and large they had the measure of each other, a real symbiotic partnership, and as the years passed they grew together like two almonds sharing one shell, with all the pleasure and pain a relationship of that nature entails. Many years later I had been leaned on to do one of those live TV interviews, travelling up to Birmingham and back. My folks had videoed it and when I went home to lunch the following Sunday they put it on for us kids to watch. Laying it on a bit thick, the lady interviewer announced me as someone who had been called one of the world's most beautiful men. I happened to turn and saw my mum and dad standing together in the doorway, catching a moment between them. I can't remember if my mother actually said, 'And why not?' She probably did, knowing her, but it was the look that said it all. They had come through thick and thin with children they were proud of and grandchildren they had lived to enjoy.

Dad always found it hard to take that I entertained such grand ideas. My childhood must have seemed princely compared to his. He told me of one occasion, just after he started work and was buying good gear for the first time. He'd at last put a lock on the door of the clothes cupboard to stop his suit 'walking'. Coming home one evening to find the table bare, he had asked his mother where his dinner was.

'It's upstairs,' was her reply.

'What's it doing up there?' he asked.

'I don't know, Tom. It's in that cupboard with the padlock on.'

You had to get him in an expansive mood for him to talk about himself. He was a man who had always kept his own counsel and was often scornful of the middle class and their values. I dread to think what he must have felt about my trying to keep up with the Joneses. A few years back, on his birthday, we met in Fortnum's and, imagining that Dad must be feeling his age a bit, I pointed out an octogenarian who was still working in the food hall. Dad was sixty-nine at the time.

I said, 'See that fella there. He's worked here for sixty years. He's eight-five. Amazing, isn't it.'

'I don't see what's amazing,' Dad retorted. 'He's never done a proper day's work in his life.'

That same afternoon I wanted to get him a pair of topsider boat shoes that wouldn't slip on ice. I was about to walk into a rather exclusive shoe shop in Bond Street. He put his hand on my arm and said, 'The old lady always used to say, "Don't walk in unless you can walk out".' He knew I hadn't been working much and it was his way of letting me know he didn't expect anything. Those Sperries were the last present I had the pleasure of buying him.

I was duly taken to Hammet's to be outfitted for grammar school. Hammet's was the only really beautiful shop I remember in Plaistow. It stood on the corner of Barking Road and Denmark Street with a curved glass window and two entrances. The name ran round both sides in a glass-covered gold leaf. It was the one shop I had never been in (it was one you couldn't walk into without being able to walk out) but had always wanted to. Hammet's specialised in trophies, medals, college scarves, presentation watches, uniforms and the like. A bell tinkled invitingly as you pushed against the polished swirl of the brass door handle that ran from bottom right to almost above my head on the left. It had that aroma I always associate with quality, but quality embellished with the patina of age; *wabi*, I think they say in Japan. The floor, polished wood of random-width planks, peeked from the sides of the Turkey carpet but it was not any old Turkey carpet. An abundance of rich muted Paisley spilled across the red field. My not-club-elegant shoes almost sank into it.

'Yes, Madam,' said Mr Hammet.

'My son, Terence,' said Mother, and then not without pride, 'needs a uniform for Plaistow Grammar.'

'Of course. You have the authorisation, Madam?'

For one moment I saw the visit fizzling out, but Mum opened her handbag. I noted it was her best one, leather, for Sunday visits, and drew out the official notification of acceptance. Mr Hammet waved it aside. 'Thank you. You do understand . . . ' He feigned embarrassment at his lack of trust.

'Well, you can't have just anybody walking in and . . . ' She paused, realising she had lost her middle-class decorum.

'Exactly,' said Mr Hammet. 'Now, if Master Terence would come this way.' He swivelled and moved across the floor as if on ball bearings through a heavy curtain on brass rings. Master Terence followed and entered what was a modern cave of Ali Baba. One whole wall racked with the feminine green and cream of Sara Bonnells, then the black and maroon, very chic, of Stratford Grammar, and where Mr Hammet was standing, the plain navy-blue of Plaistow.

'Now, Sir, long or short trousers?'

'Lo – '

'Short,' said Mum, who had joined us. I wasn't to have proper long trousers for another three years.

'Yes,' agreed Mr Hammet, slipping the tape measure from around his neck and putting it around my waist almost at the same time as picking up a pair of grey flannels from a shelf.

'Just slip these on in the fitting room, and we will get started on the blazer.'

Fitting room, good. Underpants clean, but almost threadbare, hadn't thought of that. I could hear the adults discussing my look for the next five years, maybe seven.

'You see, Mrs Stamp, the Plaistow uniform may seem a little austere but once the badge is in place . . . Ah yes, would you require the attachable variety or, if you take the blazer with the patch pocket, like this one here, we can embroider it directly on to the pocket which can be transferred to a – '

'No, this one will do fine,' I heard Mum decide, too hastily I thought.

Now what was that about 'embroidered directly . . .'

A few years back, I had a blazer made and, as the only occasion I've ever been properly entitled to wear a badge was when I attended Plaistow Grammar, I decided to re-create it. Plaistow Grammar no longer exists. It has been transformed into Cumberland High. Its airy corridors open on to the grass quadrangles, now boarded up, and its windows are covered with protective wiring. However, the present headmaster did put me in touch with an old classmate, Pete Sullivan, who had kept his original badge and he kindly lent it to me to have copied. I was dumbfounded to discover that this obviously genuine article was made of cotton and not silk as I had always remembered it to be, so strong must have been the impression I received on coming from the changing booth and finding Mr Hammet holding up my blazer with the badge in place on the top pocket. Mum was holding the tie; it was still contrasting putty and blue broad stripes in '49. It was my regalia until '52 when, on the way to making us all equal, it became just blue. That day, however, it was the finest tie I had ever seen and I was unable to wear it out although I must confess I gave it a bashing before mastering the double windsor. That double windsor came to my notice when Roy Charles Studd entered my life.

The summer of '49 was the happiest of my boyhood. Gran had been very ill, but had recovered and Mum had told me how pleased she was that Gran would see me in my uniform. It would be a good idea to go there after school and see as much of her as I could. I didn't need any second bidding, putting my arms around her eighteen-inch waist and squeezing her to me as often as I could. I had the feeling that the family knew something I didn't, but I put it from my mind.

I remember so well those first terms at grammar school. I was glowing with my success and, although I was delegated to 2D, the lowest form of the first year, I shrugged it off. I had started at the bottom before. Although I missed the hop-picking that autumn for the first time, Mum said it would be worth the sacrifice in order to have a good start at the new school. Aunt Maude had married for the second time and moved into her husband's family house, just the other side of the Cumberland Road sports ground, which the back of the school overlooked, so I used to go there for lunch when the family were in Yalding at New Barns Farm. My school report that year reflects the optimistic mood I must have been in. All excellents and no subjects below 70%, lots in the eighties and nineties. I was seventh in my form and made it to the back row. The hierarchy was different from primary school where the toughest took the desks they wanted. At Plaistow, the top of the class sat in the back right-hand corner and, as we had single rather than double desks, my position entitled me to the back left-hand corner. I was never to reside in the esteemed back row again.

At weekends during the hop harvest I would go over the Canning Town Bridge and, at a pick-up point near Howard's Hardwoods, catch a lorry that took weekend visitors to the hop fields. The driver would take me for half a crown and often squeezed me into the cabin between himself and his mate. The drive through the Blackwall Tunnel which opened on to the vistas of the Black Heath was a journey always looked forward to. The symbolism still holds. We often reached Seven Mile Lane before sunset and the real countryside began. It is hard to explain what hopping was like for us Cockneys who had no connection with the country at all apart from this annual ritual. That year, because I was being weaned, so to speak, those weekends became cherished. The

Above: The hopping holiday I missed

The.Woolpack.Inn Yalding —

lorry would pass the Woolpack pub, its monster conker tree towering outside, with strains of a piano accordion and singing reaching into us as we passed. Then we'd turn left, the wheels would bump over the varicose roots of the 'hundred-year-old pine tree'. There would be glimpses of the bulrushes on the sides of the bottomless pond where the horse and cart with drunken driver had once disappeared, and we had arrived. Fires still glowing in front of some of the huts, and the smoke drifting invisibly across the still evening was the best perfume I'd ever smelt. Only time for a few hurried glimpses at beloved landmarks before entering the paraffin-lit hut for a cup of country milk from a wide-topped bottle and to bed on that shiny straw masterpiece, the scent of which seemed to lull you to sleep in seconds. One weekend I was taken down by Dad. We caught the train on Saturday morning. I remember standing on the platform of London Bridge Station. He was wearing a dove-grey suit and wide-brimmed trilby. He looked so handsome. I knew Gran always said, 'Handsome is as handsome does,' but looking up at him I thought, if I grow up a bit like that it wouldn't half be bad.

The school in Prince Regent's Lane was well designed. If the whole of the East End had been designed by that architect, it wouldn't be the mess it is now. The school was a bungalow constructed around two open quadrangles. Access to these grass-covered rectangles was from covered walkways which skirted single blocks of classrooms on seven sides. The eighth side was the wall of the inner half of the double science corridor, composed of two blocks of laboratories with a traditional corridor between them. This arm was solely used for physics, chemistry and biology, except for the boys' washroom and, at the top end, as if an afterthought, the music room and the classroom of Form 2D. It was into this oddment that I reported on my first day, filled with hopes of academia, of eventually winding up at Oxford and rowing for the dark blues. However, it was not to be. After the first year, when my splendid grades coincided with what must have been an educational policy of going easy, catchee monkee, I was promoted to 3C, along with most of my classmates. Then the honeymoon ended. I think the last really good mark I received, apart from woodwork, was for the painting I did in the summer vacation entitled 'Swimming'. It had been assigned us as a holiday project by the art mistress, the ravishing Miss Fowler. Did I have a crush on her! Sometimes she would stand behind me while I worked, close enough for me to catch her perfume, and on those occasions when she leaned over my shoulder and her chestnut hair touched my face, the whole of my back became goosepimpled and I dreamed of being detained by her after class and forgoing my virginity in the store room with the whitewashed windows. Alas, she was to leave at the end of the second year, and became the first in what was to become a considerable list of unrequited crushes on older women who didn't initiate me into their mysteries.

My summer assignment, however, was a triumph. I chose to depict the Beckton Lido which had only luminous associations, except for the time when I had been pushed in fully clothed by Georgie Smith's younger brother, Terry, before I could swim. I was rescued soon enough by a lifeguard and given hot Bovril. Mum came and fetched me with dry clothes. I featured the incident in a corner of my painting. Mum really disliked the Chadwin Road companions and took it personally when I was made to look foolish. Her belief that I was special was not at all flexible. It was as though she feared I would be tainted by what were really only harmless urchins. The harridans of the street who intimidated other mothers cut no ice at all with her. Mrs Hughes, who lived opposite, was a huge woman with a huge family. One afternoon she came and complained at our door in a typically bombastic manner about something I had or had not done, shouting and pushing her enormous tits into our passage.

Mum didn't give an inch.

'I'll deal with my son myself, if it's needed,' and, poking her foreshortened index finger (which even my dad found disconcerting) into the top of Mrs Hughes's mammaries, she continued, 'And don't stick that bloody shelf out at me, or I'll knock it off.'

Mrs Hughes bounced back into the road as the door slammed on her ample bosom.

My painting, being a holiday homework, was fulfilled under almost ideal conditions: on the rug in front of Gran's stove, which burned cheerfully all year round, with Gran in the scullery making Silver Shred sandwiches and singing 'Little Dolly Daydreams' to herself. The six weeks, plus extra if we went hopping, lay endlessly ahead. I had all the time in the world to complete the picture. I observed the inmates of the lido through holes in the planks most days – I was only getting 1/3d a week pocket money and Saturday morning pictures took most of that. I would then walk to Barking Road where I kept my art book and Derwent Water coloured pencils and add what I had seen to my picture. These were the moments I held dear, enfolded for ever into my psyche. Moments with my gran, treasured all the more because I knew that some day I'd have to face life without her. I have always had that feeling when somebody dies that they are still here. But when she passed on I did miss the warmth of her love around me.

My picture was completed with all the detail of a master builder. It drew a juicy nine out of ten from the luscious Miss Fowler, but no invitation for the young Lowry to investigate her in art supplies. When she abandoned us it seemed the final straw. I had already started to realise that education even in the rarefied heights of grammar school consisted of lists to be memorised; lists of dates for history, lists of places for geography, lists of verbs perfect and imperfect for French, lists of tables and theorems for maths, lists of words to be spelt correctly in dictation for English, lists of symbols for chemistry. It seemed that was all there was to school, except for art, woodwork and PT, presided over by the high sadist himself, Mr Priest, always in tinted spectacles so it was difficult to see his eyes. It was hard to face that the whole of my youth would be spent incarcerated behind a desk, being persuaded, cajoled, often bullied, into doing the one thing that was alien to me. I just could not force my mind to take in all this bumf and recall it at will. Faced with information to be learned, my brain would prance like a wild horse, out of the window across the playing fields or on to the icy curls of Barbara Say or the tight folds of Kay Vincent's pencil skirt. It refused to learn anything. At the same time there was a sneaking feeling that somehow I knew better. I wanted my life to be spent with an ease, for example, that wasn't indolence; with a grace in action that didn't exclude work. Of course, it wasn't as clear as that.

I did consider asking the Reverend Willard at St Cedd's, but he'd failed my first question: 'If God made everything, who made God?' My family, all so delighted with my new status (uniform to prove it), just knew education was the way up and out. All my classmates were giving it a try. I went through the motions – but my reaction persisted. Release came partially through the portals of Fairbairn and Mansfield House Boys' Club and a hero the likes of which I hadn't happened on before.

Five

FAIRBAIRN'S PALACE

Above: Richard's turn to ride the tiger

Fairbairn's Palace

Fairbairn was the grandest place I'd ever been in. It was a three-storeyed building, officially opened in July 1900. It had been the brainchild of a Reverend Fairbairn, its first principal. It later joined forces with Mansfield House and became Fairbairn and Mansfield House University Settlement, Fairbairn being for boys aged seven to fourteen and Mansfield for members aged fourteen to twenty-one. The central idea was to give kids in the depressed areas of Canning Town and Plaistow some recreation, and keep them off the streets when the pocket money ran out. When I was signed up, Sir Ian Horobin was the warden. He was responsible for finding the donations which kept the place going. He wore a pince-nez, had been in a Japanese prison camp during the War, and was formidable. The heavy glass-panelled doors were opened at six-thirty p.m. and we crowded around outside in anticipation. Inside, to the left, was a counter and a cloakroom where our membership cards were checked and overcoats taken from those who had them. Although the severe red-brick façade was all that was visible from the Barking Road entrance, inside the building opened out like an accordion, stretching the whole depth of the block and backing on to Avenons Road.

As I had joined the club primarily to learn to 'take care of myself', Ethel had put me down for gymnastics on Mondays and boxing on Wednesdays. That first Monday I walked down the corridor in a leisurely fashion, blinking rapidly and trying to take in all the luxury, while all the other boys pushed ahead of me, their Blakied boots clattering metallically on the marble floor. It wasn't marble, but a kind of concrete with embedded stone chips and sufficiently burnished for me to assume it was. None of the corridors were straight, nor were the stairs; they were all curved. So there wasn't a stop and start feel about the place; everything just rolled into everything else. I passed a wide staircase leading off to the left; it followed the sweep of the wall which had a large stone plaque halfway up: 'You are not your own. You were bought at a great price.' I was keen to climb the inviting stairs, but followed the others down some steps and through the swing doors into a massive gymnasium.

It was a magnificent affair and incorporated a full two floors in height. Climbing ropes hung from its twenty-foot-high ceiling, and the wall bars along the length of two sides were all of twelve feet. An L-shaped gallery ran along the top of two sides, giving access to the boxing area which was recessed in one corner above the wall bars. From the floor of the gym I could see the ropes of a ring and punching bags. I could hear boys already trying to knock the daylights out of each other. The gym instructor ushered me through another set of swing doors to the changing rooms which looked just like any other at first glance, with rows of clothes hooks and benches, but beyond an arch to the left was a much bigger area which had as its centrepiece a sunken threepenny-bit-shaped stone bath easily large enough to hold a junior football squad. For an embryonic clean freak who lived without a bathroom and was dependent on a tin bath coming in on Friday nights with only enough hot water for one filling, this encounter was rather like a land-locked duck coming upon water in middle age. Lying up to my chin in luxurious steaming water after the games session in the gym, my head resting on a section of the octagonal surround, I thought, this is it, someone's rubbed Aladdin's lamp.

It didn't take me long to learn the ropes. After one punishing session in the boxing ring, I talked to a few other boys my age and got the hang of things. The old hands used the place like the gents of St James's use their clubs. On the first floor at the top of the semi-circular stairs was another curved corridor. Off to the right was the secretary's office, a snooker salon with three full-size tables used by the older boys, but to the left was a spacious lounge area on several levels. Once through the doors the atmosphere became warm and inviting; the wooden steps were wide and angled to follow the shape of the room which was kidney-shaped on split levels. Small tables and chairs dotted the top section. Two ladies behind a corner counter administered to our needs with cooked snacks, Tizer, buns, tea and coffee. To the right, also on the top level, a banquette of seats overlooked the gymnasium through a wall of windows. The sunken floor, which was the main area, was also made of wood, like a dance floor. It may have been intended as such, but it was mostly used by boys rushing to get to the gallery and the woodwork room on the other side of the lounge. We weren't supposed to run anywhere once inside the club; it was one of the rules along with a ban on smoking. The club was organised with few staff considering the number of boys who used it, the idea being that we policed it ourselves; Fairbairn's theory was that if we had really good surroundings provided for us, we would appreciate them and feel responsible. While I was there this was proved to be the case; no boy reported another for having a quick puff or trotting along the corridor, but there was never any vandalism or graffiti and few cigarette butts were dropped on the floor.

Two brothers, both handsome along the lines of Cornel Wilde, straight away made a big impression on me with their exotic clothes. Both had sallow complexions with dark hair; they might have been of Greek or Maltese extraction. They often wore dark shirts, bottle-green and maroon, not with light ties like spivs, but a similar shade so they appeared tieless until viewed close up. I was particularly struck when the younger one – all of thirteen – turned up one evening in a pale greeny-blue shirt buttoned to the neck without a tie. Along the points of the collar was a single line of zig-zag green embroidery. It took weeks of looking in shop windows to discover where he'd found it, and then it was way outside my budget.

Upstairs from the lounge was the woodwork room, again outfitted with all the tools imaginable, including a circular saw, an iron lathe which nobody knew how to work, and a wood lathe, which I soon mastered, and successfully made lamp standards, and a proper child's swing just like in the park, for my brothers. Dad put heavy hooks in the door frame between the living-room and the scullery and it was well used by both Chris and Richard. It was one of my more impressive handiworks.

In one corner of the woodwork room was a short flight of stairs which led up to a door through which we were not supposed to go. One evening, finishing the class a bit after eight, the instructor left, entrusting me to switch off the lights and slam the door. I saw a light coming from under the door, and heard voices on the other side. I climbed the stairs and knocked, figuring I'd use the excuse of being left in charge to enquire whether everything was all right. The door was opened by an old man, or rather he appeared old at first glance, but as my eyes adjusted to the bright light I saw that he was just made up to appear so, with a bald wig glued to his forehead. Seeing my curiosity, he invited me in. It was a rather long narrow room, like a ship's galley. One side had a wide shelf at table height, with mirror panels against the wall the length of the room above it. The sections of mirror were framed with bare, frosted light bulbs every eighteen inches or so. There were chairs in front of the shelf, and on one of these some clothes hung; the shelf in front was littered with what was apparently make-up, but of a type I hadn't seen before. Sticks wrapped in silver paper, varying from the size of a pencil to the width of a cigar. Most of them lay untidily in and around a Havana cigar box. There was a tin of cream, a round box of powder, a big powder puff and short strands of rope, one of which had been separated at one end and looked like hair. I took all this in in a flash but the aroma that filled the place seemed almost familiar, although I couldn't think when I had smelt it before.

'You like my greasepaint?' the man said.

It turned out that he was the leading man in the Wanstead and Woodford Dramatic Society. They were using the Fairbairn House Theatre for three performances that weekend. Dress rehearsal that night. He was very nice with me, that fella, although he didn't introduce himself. He gave me some coffee, made with milk, from his Thermos flask and chatted to me while I watched him finish off his make-up, putting spirit gum from a bottle on to his upper lip and affixing tufts of crêpe hair directly on top to make a tash. I felt so at home in that room that for a long time afterwards I harboured a secret desire to become a make-up man in the movies. When it was time for him to start rehearsal, he asked me my name, commenting, 'That's a *good* name,' and offering to leave a ticket for me at reception for the Saturday matinée.

'Five o'clock, don't forget.'

Forget! My life had just changed, and I hadn't even known there was a theatre at Fairbairn House. Although I trotted directly home, my mum wanted to know where I'd been. As it was almost ten o'clock, I couldn't work it out. My time spent in the dressing room must have flashed by. It had seemed like moments.

The next day at five o'clock the curtain went up on *Fumed Oak*. It proved to be a Noël Coward one-acter, about a middle-aged henpecked husband who finally turns on his wife and daughter. I thought it was all just brilliant. It was the first time I had seen a straight play. In fact, it was the first time I'd been to the theatre, unless you count going to the Troxy to see Derek Roy in pantomine.

The theatre at Fairbairn, although rarely used (the club didn't have a resident company), was a little jewel. A fully equipped working house with wall switchboard, a full contingent of lights, boxes of gels, flies, spacious wings, prompt and O.P. side and a luxurious intimate auditorium which must have sat two hundred. A perfect spot for an aspiring thespian to tread the boards. I never did, although I tried almost everything else. I haunted the place whenever a company set foot inside it. Picking up info like a sponge, I reckon that by the time I left Fairbairn I could have stagemanaged a production on my own. I did get on the stage once in an audition a company gave there. I told a story of how, as a small boy when sent up to bed early, I had covered myself in Pond's Vanishing Cream, believing it would render me invisible, and came downstairs nude to join a party. I did get a lot of laughs but I was still small for my age and obviously there wasn't much call for twelve year olds. At that first matinée I saw an actress called Hilary Lago play the plain daughter. She was to turn up later playing Hermia in *A Midsummer Night's Dream* during her final term at Plaistow Grammar. I was so knocked out by *Fumed Oak* that I left the theatre when the interval curtain came down, never realising that a bill of one-act plays generally consists of two. I'm afraid I was too unknowing to congratulate that actor or even to thank him for my front-row seat. So, sir, if you played the husband in *Fumed Oak* opposite Hilary Lago at Fairbairn and Mansfield House Theatre in the early 1950s and recognise yourself, thank you. I owe you one.

I was illuminated by those evenings at the club. But by day I toiled, trying to keep my mind from wandering off like an ox into the long grass. We were exposed to no enlightened teachers and few with charisma. There was an English teacher called Miss Baron whom I rather took to after she read us *The Wind in the Willows* one term. There was also a lady biology teacher who came to school on a big motorbike. I heard she had a crush on Geoff Duke, and she seemed rather fun, but we didn't get her. A Miss Trollop tried in vain to persuade us to speak correctly, or 'proper' as we called it. I wish I had paid more attention to her. We had singing and music only in the first year and then our class band vanished. Apart from the forementioned, most of the other teachers – like 'Butch' Priest, who would set about boys at the drop of an argument; Govier, who was employed to frighten kids into not learning French; and 'Killer' Ward, who would get in a rage and hurl chalk at dimwits like me, often misaiming and hitting innocent swots – would have been better suited to a borstal institution, in my opinion.

My mum used to say, 'Schooldays are the best days of your life.' I often thought, if it gets worse than this when I leave school I'll kill myself. I tried to keep fit, mainly from the gym I did in the evening.

At school I did enough to pass Priest's sadistic eye unnoticed and I succeeded pretty well until I had my appendix removed and was sent away to Sherbourne to convalesce. This was more because we slept three in a room and were considered underprivileged rather than really in need. Anyway, I went, and a very interesting time I had too, but I was away from school for over a month and when I returned Priest suddenly realised I had been missing. He got it into his head that I had been malingering and really kept coming down on me hard. I wouldn't back off and he kept on. I used to stay awake at night thinking of ways that I could maim him without getting killed in the process. In '74 I went back to the school building to open a fête. If that damn Priest wasn't still there! The headmaster introduced me to him. Would you believe that bugger tried to stare me out through his kinky tinted specs? It was all I could do not to spit in his face.

Looking back, it seems I didn't have a male figure to look up to. My grandfathers were hospitalised or away at sea. I was the eldest

Above: The illustrious Form 4C

grandchild, with girl cousins. My dad was distant with me, and my Uncle Harry, whom I thought the world of, was too eccentric for me to identify with. He escaped from his wood machinist's bench by long-distance cycling and winning every gold medal available at ballroom dancing. As for the local kids, the rough ones were too rough, the middle-class ones too floppy. Without realising it, I had never had a best friend, and my only idols were on the silver screen. According to some pundits of the physical aspects of human nature, man, like most animals, goes through a homosexual phase. This happens in the early teens and can be seen in crushes that girls have on their prefects, boys have on team captains and so on. It sometimes extends to actual sexual play, but in most cases this doesn't happen and, if bridged without trauma, it can make for a fuller sexual appreciation later in life. It is also thought that if the sexual urge isn't repressed when at its strongest between the ages of fourteen and twenty-one, mental sexual obsession isn't prolonged into old age. Well, that's how the theory goes. I didn't know any of this when I came across Roy Studd, and I'd better say straight away that the charming, but very level-headed Roy probably didn't have an inkling of any of my feelings. Even if he had, it probably wouldn't have made any difference to him. He was that sort of guy.

When Mum had signed me up at Fairbairn, none of the other kids from Chadwin Road had wanted to know. This was the first real break I made with the working-class section of my patch, and it meant that I entered club life on my own. Of course, once initiated I met kids of my own age who lived only a few streets away but, because they attended different schools and didn't belong to the local gangs, I had never before come across Teddy Debell and Colin Stevens to name a few. Colin was my age and Teddy a year younger, but so physically mature that most of the time I considered him older than me. He was good-looking with large, strong features and a shock of dark brown hair, a forelock of which always fell over one eye. He had an older brother, Brian, who was blond, and who we both felt was a bit wet. They lived in a sizeable house in Brock Road which had a bathroom and real stained glass in the front door. Mr Debell, his father, was a sailor and middle-weight boxing champion of the Navy. On one electric occasion when a summer fun-fair came to Beckton Park, he took up a challenge thrown from the boxing booth to all comers in the crowd, but was denied a fight when at close quarters the tattooed carnies got a good butchers at his cauliflower ear. Teddy took after him. I guessed he was what in those days would have passed as a rascal. Always good for a laugh, preferably accompanied by a bit of trouble or danger. He had also been enrolled at Fairbairn to learn 'how to use himself', but being no muggins he soon located other outlets for using himself. We came across each other in the gym class. His mate was Colin, who lived a few doors along from him also in Brock Road. We had all gone to Tolgate but didn't become friendly until Fairbairn.

We all soaked in the threepenny-bit-bath after class and Colin showed us his one rather lengthy pubic hair of which he was suitably proud. Neither Teddy nor I had anything to show, but that didn't stop Teddy assuring his chum, 'Oh, you should be getting "the feeling" soon.'

We would walk home together, stopping at the fish shop in Denmark Street to buy a bag of chips and a pickled onion. Or, if things were not eventful enough, Teddy would open the door of the off-licence just enough to keep the entry bell ringing and make the owner charge out into a deserted shop.

My mother had tried to encourage a friendship between me and the son of the local vicar, the Reverend Willard, and I once went to play with him in the palatial garden of their manse, which was bigger than the churchyard. It amazed me that one house could have a garden that big, with a paddling pool, fruit trees and a vine that bore tiny black grapes. I spent a whole day in that garden, ending with high tea in the vicarage; not just jam sandwiches, but proper sandwiches, tinned salmon and cucumber, dark brown fruit cake with cherries and a tea strainer which sat in its own little silver holder. The Reverend's wife seemed rather taken aback as she observed my habit of pouring my tea into the saucer and blowing on it before slurping it down.

'What is the cup for, Terence?' she asked.

'To pour it into the saucer with.'

I wasn't asked back, even though Ethel had me screaming away in that choir for years. The bonding between the delicate John Willard and me wasn't a natural one and Teddy and Colin were my first real mates. There were never any fights between us – I suppose we were too different for any real rivalry to arise. Colin was competent at every kind of game; from street events to billiards and snooker, he always seemed to know the rules. Teddy just muscled his way and I tried to think things through; none of us had any desire to win or be better than the other.

There were two plane trees in Brock Road, quite old I would imagine, but because the Council pruned them every year their growth was contained and they never appeared to change. There were no low branches, which made them difficult to climb, but I persevered tenaciously and after a time could haul myself into both, the second one being the hardest to negotiate. This second tree was near a house where a very attractive girl named Megan lived, a neighbour of Teddy's and almost the same age. The prospect of viewing the lovely Megan unobserved had Teddy up the tree quick enough, and soon it was summer headquarters for the trio. Colin invented a way of tapping into the telephone wires which passed through the branches and, although we couldn't interject our own comments, even to be party to a telephone was a thrill. There is something peculiarly private about the top of a tree which commands respect. I often have this feeling as a weekend guest in a country house when my room overlooks trees.

But a town tree, which will accommodate a body unseen, was the next best thing to being able to render myself invisible. I learnt to climb and drop from those trees so adroitly that, unless my passage was being watched from behind lace curtains by the sharp-eyed Mrs Solly, I could disappear as if into another dimension, which in truth I felt I did. Mrs Solly had a daughter, Ivy, who was to grow up into a real piece. The Solly household was in Chadwin but adjacent to Brock Road, and therefore within my viewing scope. I became familiar with the Solly girls' comings and goings. It was before the stress of puberty and could be defined as voyantism rather than voyeurism. When I was in the tree with my mates it was just a giggle, but when alone whatever I was observing seemed endowed with a special quality, so that even the behaviour of local cats and dogs took on surreal dimensions. I knew that what I was doing was a bit strange but it seemed important; it was somewhere I could be on my own, to read, to look.

Of course it didn't occur to me that my very looking was different at these times. I just needed a secret, and having a secret gave me power. Born and brought up in town, with rare trips to the country and its more apparent seasons, I was all the more aware of the streets and their atmosphere. Certain streets I liked and felt happy with; in others I felt uneasy, and these I would avoid, even when it meant taking a longer route on errands (as a child I was a real loafer and wouldn't walk if there was the slightest possibility of a bus). Today I still have automatic green routes I opt for when on foot.

I was in awe of Johnny Straffon, whose garden backed on to the side of ours. Johnny had so much front that he wouldn't go to his primary school unless his mother wheeled him in a push-chair. He must have been seven or eight before he started walking like the rest of us. Mrs Straffon kindly let me use their garden wall to get in our back door when Mum was out, and one day after I had just started at grammar school I came home to find neither Mum nor Daisy Straffon in. As it was winter, I decided to go to Barking Road to visit my gran. I had 3d in my pocket to take the 699 trolley. There was a craze at the time for shining up ha'pennies and pennies with dust from red house bricks. I filled our porch with indentations collecting dust for this alchemy. At work on my pennies – I always carried some brick dust granules in my hanky – while waiting for the trolley, I saw a couple walking towards me.

The girl was small – petite, my mum would have said – the guy tall and slim. They were loosely holding hands. As they came closer, I could see there was something very different about them. They were certainly 'not one of us'. She was impossibly pretty, with shortish curly hair and delicate chiselled features. She turned her face up to his as they strolled; her lashes long, her eyes bright, she could have been Gene Tierney's younger sister, but more vulnerable. The man was also startling; his skin was as if tanned, he had wide-set eyes, a sort of slate-blue – a colour I hadn't come across before – and his hair, long for that time, was prematurely grey with white sideboards. He was walking languidly; his long legs seemed to drift so as to keep apace with hers. He was wearing a heavy gabardine raincoat with a buckleless tie-belt and a pair of crêpe-soled suede shoes, cobalt blue. The soles were thick and made him seem even taller, but not like the local spivs and drones who often wore creepers. I felt sure the couple would stop and wait at the bus stop so I would be able to examine them more closely, get a chance to overhear their conversation. But it was not to be. Absorbed in each other, they passed the small boy lounging unnoticed at the bus stop, enveloping him briefly in their aura and her scent, which smelled like wallflowers. I puzzled for days about how their visitation came to pass. I knew the neighbourhood, I knew they were not locals of my patch. They had come from Prince Regent's Lane, north of the park where the public library was. Beyond that it became rough territory, with only the speedway and finally the docks to distinguish Custom House. I was never to solve the mystery, but for years the tap of the slingback shoes, which drew my eye to the silky heel and dainty ankles, haunted my waking dreams, although it was difficult even to imagine this delicate creature voluntarily revealing more of herself. I finally decided that I would like to grow up like him and marry someone like her. I began to urge my height.

Six

PRESENTS BEFORE CHRISTMAS

Above: My first double-breasted

Presents Before Christmas

One evening at Fairbairn, after gymnastics, I had been comparing my physique with the other boys in the bath. A lot of them were taller and broader than me and most of them had noticeable pubic hair. I was twelve years old and we had just broken up at school for the Easter holiday. All of us had been duly weighed and measured. I was appalled to discover that even when really stretching up I was still only four feet eleven. So, rather than being elated by the holiday ahead, I felt dejected, so small and puny beside my contemporaries who all seemed to be sporting bits of fluff, like trumpet players, on their upper lips. Lenny Pearce, whose folks had a café in Forest Gate, was already body-building, and Murkoff in the 'A' form, whose dad owned the ice-cream shop near the Rathbone Street Market, had a real blue shadow; it was rumoured that he shaved every day with an electric razor. It had been consoling to hear Dr Brandreth remark to Ethel, when he extricated a planter's wart from the sole of my foot, that I had fine big feet and would probably be tall one day, but that day seemed permanently fixed in the future. Conscious that Dad was only just as tall as her (she never wore high heels when they went out together), Mum was always going on about men needing to be a certain height to be proficient ballroom dancers. Uncle Harry, also on the short side, had every gold medal ever cast for dancing, including a clutch for South American and *paso doble*. He confided to me that his height didn't stop him getting dances (he gave dances a rather ambiguous stress) but it did limit his choice of regular partners. It certainly wasn't part of my plan to have my choices limited. Mum said children often took after their grand-parents, and Grandfather Perrott had been tall and slim, but my looks were proving more and more like the Stamp side of the family, and Grandfather Stamp was even shorter than my dad. I was deep in these sort of onanistic introversions, wondering how I could become school high-jump champion and get my name in the record books, when I heard an excellent Dean Martin impersona-tion coming down the stairs from the top snooker room: 'How do you speak to an angel?'

As it was unusual to hear any singing in the club, or anywhere at all except in the pub, let alone so confidently and well executed, I waited in the vestibule to see who came with the voice. Sure enough, down the curve of the staircase strolled a boy, older than myself. His voice had obviously broken; he was having no trouble with Dean's low register, at any rate. There was a group of three or four guys just behind him, like courtiers in attendance. Except this was no gang leader; this was royalty and the crooner was a young king.

Many years later in Poona, I came out of a shop called Dorabjee & Co., where I'd had some coffee ground, to find a big herd of water buffalo being slowly herded down Molalina Road. They were headed by a male with bigger horns than the others. As he drew level to where I stood, he looked at me. I have travelled a lot in hot countries, seen a lot of brown-eyed buffalo and eaten a lot of curd made from their milk, but I have never encountered another with eyes like this chap. They were bright turquoise and steady; they reminded me of Roy Studd that first night as he flashed me a grin on his way to wherever he was going.

The pain which I often had in my stomach became worse during the term between Easter and the long summer break. I would writhe about on the rug in front of the fire and the only relief was from almost boiling water administered to me by Mum. The first visit to Doctor Brandreth at his surgery in Cumberland Road secured some ineffectual white peppermint-tasting medicine. The second visit was followed by a trip on the 175 bus – we caught one with open stairs, my favourite. It seemed a good omen, but it wasn't. Three doctors were not sure, but the fourth, who must have held seniority, pronounced my condition to be 'a grumbling appendix', so it was arranged to 'have me in' and 'whip it out'. I was very frightened, and also deep down I felt it was just not right. I cried on the bus home. The medical profession knew that the thing grumbling in my tum was some kind of divine clumsiness that would be better out than in. No matter that in the Orient that same appendage is viewed as a valve which houses unwanted gas until it can be emitted usefully aiding a bowel movement. As nobody at 124 knew anything about the Chinese, let alone their sophisticated medical system, the little barometer was cut out and the cause of my aches driven deeper, starting a spiral which was to have repercussions for a long time. In fact, there was a little shop opposite the florist's by the Abbey Arms which today would be called a health shop. The window was filled with dishes of exotic specimens; sunflower seeds, sun-dried bananas and the like. I often hung around there in the evening, wondering what those dark brown banana things, honey and wheatgerm would taste like. It was

open on Saturday mornings so I could have gone in after the
Balaam Street baths, but I was always drawn to the blacksmith's
shop in New Barn Street and stood in the whitewashed doorway
for hours just to be near the glowing forge and the reek of burning
hooves. However, instead of getting plugged into the naturopathy
on my doorstep, I checked into Poplar Hospital where I spent a
forlorn week only cheered by Mum and Dad throwing rolled-up
American comics on to the balcony of the first floor ward from
where I watched the traffic and the East India Dock on the other
side of the road. A fortnight after I came home, Mum and I had a
letter from the hospital to go and meet the local health officer in the
Almoner's Office. It was to be decided whether or not I would be
sent away for convalescence. What swung it in my favour was that
my two brothers and I all slept in the same room. As this pro-
posed holiday didn't clash with hopping and meant whole weeks
away from school, I was all for it. No outlay on our side met with
Ethel and Tom's approval, so I was packed off on the train to
Shoeburyness.

I have always loved trains, and in those days they were steam,
with windows that opened. I was in my element. Travelling alone
never presented any problems – I preferred it. I have met
'sensitives' who feel that the atmosphere of trains increases their
powers of extra-sensory perception, but I just found the steel-on-
steel motion and the repetitious sounds enlivening and soothing.
I'd become more interested in girls and was travelling in my
Sunday suit, double-breasted, bitter-chocolate-brown serge with a
cream shirt and bottle-green tie, which I figured might catch the
eye of some knowing fellow traveller of the opposite sex.

A month previously Mum had encouraged me to go to Herbert's
School of Dancing at the Boleyn end of the Barking Road. Herbert
Saunders, the proprietor, was a portly, effeminate man who spoke a
bit like Frankie Howerd. At the first class several timid customers
who wouldn't find a partner, myself included, were twirled around
the ballroom by Herbert himself. Herbert was obviously posh, with
his buffed finger-nails and hand-benched shoes. It was no accident
that he had pitched his dance academy in this part of the East End.
He had a great deal of charm, and his being a Martha rather than
an Arthur didn't present any threat to us pigs' ears who were intent
on becoming silk purses. He soon sorted me out, telling me I would
have a dancer's figure when I matured ('matured' being accompa-

nied by a wicked lift of one eyebrow) and that I should have a private lesson with his lady assistant. It would be gratis to see how I made out. This assistant was a splendid creature, good-looking with shoulder-length auburn hair which she wore upswept at both sides, so the curl could only be seen on top. On the day of my trial lesson she was wearing silver strap shoes with small Cuban heels which just urged the slope of her rump so it was more noticeable through her silk frock. After one-two-threeing alongside her around the sprung maple floor, she gathered me into her arms and encouraged me to lead her. Almost instantly, the feel of her thighs through the silk against my legs gave me such a hard-on that it would have been tough enough to walk as though nothing was happening, let alone to waltz. Trying to keep a blasé look on my face – about the only part of my body I had any control over – I allowed myself to be Victor Sylvestered around until the music ended. While my instructress changed the record, I tried to adjust my trousers to look laid back. I expected that the gramophone would be turned off, and I would be asked to leave. I couldn't see how she could not have noticed my misplaced enthusiasm. But the next record started – 'If you were the only girl in the world' – and I tried to delay the embarrassment of the waltz by asking questions about timing, while looking at my shoes and succeeding only in gaping at her ankles which made things even worse. Every time I hear that tune, I think of my first dogged attempt at ballroom dancing. Needless to say, there were no more private lessons at Herbert's for Terence. Indeed, it was only many years later, with a teacher much younger than myself, that I finally mastered those wonderful rituals.

As the train pulled into Shoeburyness Station, I began to feel at home. The railway station had been built before we settled for functional ugliness, and it slotted neatly into my mixed picture of Nutwood, the landscape created by Alfred Bestall for his Rupert Bear character. My mother had somehow scraped together half a crown for those annuals so that I would find one at the bottom of my bed on Christmas morning. At Christmases when family finances could not stretch to include the coveted publication, and I had to make do with the other contents of my sock – generally a Cox's Orange Pippin or a Russet, a tangerine, several Brazil nuts and a new penny or silver threepenny bit – I depended upon the erratic goodwill of a boy called Lenny Crump. His dad was a policeman and they were better off than us. On days when street games were rained off, we took refuge in the Crumps' air raid shelter where we *aficionados* could read ole Lenny's Rupert collection to our heart's delight by torchlight and candlelight.

My dad, by the way, didn't approve of the Bear. Mum once caught him surreptitiously stuffing my Rupert literature into the dustbin. Dad wanted me to read more masculine material, *Wizard* or *Hotspur*. My own ravishment by Nutwood and its inhabitants was total. Pong-Ping, Bill Badger and the wilful Tigerlily were as real to me as the Beckton slag heaps and the debris-strewn bomb sites where we played. Myths about invisible cloaks and Jinn who travelled on thunderclouds seemed entirely reasonable to me. Although Rupert's adventures are fantastic and dreamlike, their background is real and recognisable. Spotting a shining conker or suddenly smelling burning leaves were richer experiences for me because I could recognise them as ingredients in the curious perfection of Bestall's Nutwood. Even a mundane object like my own eiderdown took on a special significance because it resembled the one that Rupert was tucked-up under by his long-suffering mum at the end of each adventure. Quite a time after weaning myself off picture books, I tried to acquire a live bear cub from the pet shop in Harrods but my flatmate wouldn't hear of it. My flatmate, known to his old mates as 'Mo' Micklewhite, later went on to fortune and celebrity as Michael Caine, but that's a different story. 'Mo' fixed on me his now famous 'cobra' look when I reported that I had already put down a cash deposit on the bear cub which, I added cajolingly, was just the sweetest little fella he would ever see, and no mistake. 'Mo' was not persuaded.

'It's a bear,' he pointed out with his unfailing South London logic, 'and they bloody well grow up.'

Well, I could scarcely fault him on that, blast him – he'd probably had a bear to cuddle as a kid and got it over with. Anyway, bang went my fantasy of cruising along the King's Road in my XK120 with the entrancing animal by my side.

Every time my life took a new turn, I had a habit of visualising some great happening which would sweep away the endless making do of our daily existence. The more time that passed without there being a break in the web, the more time I spent in pipe dreams so vivid that my picture of real life was often smudged, and I missed the significance. But this was not so at the convalescent home. On arrival, my own clothes were taken from me, including my brown double-breasted. I was kitted out in the home's clothes. They were not a uniform, far from it, but an extremely eclectic collection, like the contents of a second-hand schmatah shop down Petticoat Lane, except nothing was hanging up; the store room was big and airy, with all the windows covered by shelves up to the ceiling and on these shelves pile upon pile of folded gear. I was given a pair of winceyette pyjamas with very faded stripes, and two towels, one small, one large. Also a pair of khaki shorts and sandals, the enclosed leather type with an Alice band button strap. You couldn't have got me into them at home, but I had to admit they were comfortable. I was told to choose a jersey (sweater, the matron called it) myself. I picked a pink and purple knitted number with a zig-zag design which had run a bit. Nobody would miss me in that! I was asked if I had any sweets – I didn't. It seems they subtracted half of everyone's stock so everybody got a handful after lunch. The matron meant dinner, well the meal at midday. We slept in rooms like hospital wards; these were built around the extremities of the main building with glass ceilings and large windows looking on to the grounds. We each had a bed and a cupboard with a lamp on it which was our 'space' so to speak, although we were not encouraged to hang around the bed or use it during the day. Beds were made while we ate breakfast and remained spick and span until lights out at nine o'clock.

The table lamp was a revelation. I could read for an hour and just switch off the light without getting out of bed. I decided I'd write to Mum and tell her about it, not that we had much space at home for a table to put one on. At night it was wonderful to look at the sky through glass, or watch the rain. It was almost as good as those rare occasions which warranted a fire in our bedroom at home – like Christmas Eve, or if one of us was sick – when I could watch the shadows making the ceiling friendly; these were moments of such security and contentment that I felt on the threshold of unknown bliss. Another revelation at the convalescent home was the dressing-gown. I had never had one before, but nobody would ever have guessed it the way I flashed around in the one they gave me. It was a blue and grey design, like a tartan with some colours missing, and although it felt like a cheap blanket it had shawl lapels and a silk cord with tassels. I imagined it made me look like Cary Grant; it certainly made me feel like him. I would lie on the bedcovers in my pyjamas and dressing-gown looking up through the glass, my life stretching out in front of me filled with starlight and dreamed-of riches.

Different nurses would come round to switch off our lights and say goodnight but one of them, Nurse Grace, would actually kiss us goodnight. The boy who had the bed to my right was called Freddy and was rather ugly like a monkey. He came from Wapping where his dad fried crisps for a living. Freddy was rather proud of this and referred to himself as the 'whopper from Wapping' although he was older and smaller than me. When Nurse Grace bid us goodnight, he made a meal of it, once actually putting his arms and legs around her as she stooped over him. She calmly disentangled herself without making any reprimand. I watched from my bed, listening to the starchy sound of her outfit as she pulled back his bedclothes and manoeuvred him underneath them. Deep down I knew I was jealous of the little whopper from Wapping, both because of his nerve and because of the intimacy he could steal from Grace. She was well named, being endowed with a graceful-ness which made it appear that she was always in control of her body and the space around it. Her blonde hair was cut in a poodle, which was all the go at the time, and she had big dark eyes which looked almost black unless seen really close. Her figure was neat too, and one of those wide elastic waspy waist-belts, which none of the other nurses wore, encircled it and entranced me. There was something about her eyes – the way she looked at you – that was naughty. She wasn't wanton – I couldn't have taken the liberties that Freddy took. But there were times when I found her looking at me across the dining-room or on our daily outing to the beach, when I had the feeling that she just knew about me, about guys. As if we had no secrets from her. And she was girlish; although in her late twenties or early thirties, there was just something about her that was staying young. We were all a bit smitten by her. The boy who slept to my left and came from Wembley where he said they grew grapes in the public park – I didn't believe him – certainly was. He confessed it gave him the horn just looking at her.

'Horn?' I asked.

'Yeah, you know, when it gets big and goes all stiff.'

'Oh, you mean she gives you the jack.'

'Yeah, that's it, specially when I look at her deaf and dumb.'

'The bottle is something,' I agreed.

'Bottle?'

I let him stay mystified for a moment.

'Yeah, bottle, bottle and glass.'

He grinned, revealing a broken front tooth, and savoured the new slang as though matching it with the object of discussion. I felt deflated, another rival for Grace's attention, and I remember thinking that if I ever broke my tooth I'd get a gold bit put in it like a pirate. After sweet hand-out on Friday, some of the inmates left, Freddy among them. I'd grown to like him. I went to the front gates to wave him on his way. He looked a bit down and kept glancing back as though expecting something. The bed Freddy had occupied stayed empty that night. I told the boy from Wembley, Mark I think his name was, that I felt Freddy hadn't been in a hurry to leave. Mark said, 'Probably better off here. You got no idea how some of these families live. There's a kid on the other side who told me they sleep four in a bed, one bed! The two boys at one end and the sisters at the other. Squalid!'

Squalid, yeah, I thought, that's why I got a free holiday. It suddenly all made sense, the weekly shower rota at Tolgate which I had always gleefully put my hand up for. The monthly hair examination with the fine combs by the school nurse. No bathroom at home, not even a lavatory indoors, a toilet as they called it here. The chipped lino, cold to the feet, throughout our house. I suppose it was squalid, and that explained why we never had guests. I could never have mates in to play. I don't remember anybody with the exception of the immediate family and the insurance man ever coming into our house. Dad just didn't want anybody. Mum must have been ashamed. As I now was. But having a word for it somehow reinforced my resolve. That night I didn't sleep much. I was busy thinking how I could lift myself out of it, albeit by my own shoelaces, and then the family.

At breakfast the next morning, the object of my crush was leaning against the door frame into the kitchen. I was heaping brown sugar on to my Rice Krispies, hoping to get seconds from the bowl in the middle of the table before the whole lot vanished, when I noticed Grace looking directly at me. She was holding one hand just below her chin while she scratched it with her other hand. But it wasn't a scratch like with an itch or a gnat bite; it was slower, more deliberate. She would stop, wait a moment, start again, but not looking at her hands. I swallowed the remains of my snap crackle pop and concentrated my eyes on her. I watched her hands; it seemed she was telling me something. There was a bump, perhaps a small wart, that she was rubbing on her right hand. Her hands I noticed were rather small, the nails although clipped were long. Not filbert-shaped like Aunt Maude's, but nice. Although she kept looking at me, she wasn't staring; there was a sort of smile in her eyes, as though she was remembering a funny joke, which acted as a veil between us. Suddenly she blinked, and I felt her focus on me. She smiled, span round and went into the kitchen. I didn't catch sight of her again that day. That afternoon Mark and I walked around the gardens; they weren't highly cultivated but there were many flowers I hadn't come across before. I found some large poppies in full bud and, by gently prising open the petal coverings, could see what colour the flower would be when it bloomed. That night no nurse seemed to be coming on the rounds so I switched off my light and must have fallen asleep. I was woken up by her face very close to mine. She was whispering something like, 'So you didn't wait for me tonight, eh?'

I tried to say that I thought perhaps she wasn't coming but she pressed a small finger to my mouth and said, with lips right against my ear so it sent a shiver through my body, 'It's all right – forgive you this time.'

There was a moment when nothing happened, but I could feel her breath; it was warm and even. I didn't move. Then she said, 'You want to help me tomorrow with the laundry?'

I nodded and said, 'Yes.' She must have drawn away. I heard her footsteps moving across the polished cardinal-red tiles. My ear felt as though it was as red as the floor.

The next morning the whole episode was like part of a dream; by lunch-time I still hadn't seen Nurse Grace. I dallied in the sweet queue. Perhaps I had just imagined it. I went over the whole thing. The sister sorted out some toffees and, seeing it was me, said, 'Ah, Terence, you're helping Nurse Grace in the laundry, if you don't mind missing the beach?'

'No, no,' I stammered. Missing the beach! I would have missed a lot more to have Nurse Grace's company for an hour. I mooched around the ward while Mark from Wembley was grabbing his swimming togs from his locker.

'Come on, slow coach,' he shouted, 'they're all leaving.'

'Oh, I'm not going today. I've got to do some sort of job.' I set my face into an expression of being hard done by.

'Bad luck. See you later then.'

I listened to the line of boarders shouting and whistling their way towards the sea and then it became very quiet. I headed for the laundry which wasn't a laundry at all. It was the store room where they kept all the clothes we were issued with on arrival. The door was closed so I knocked. I heard Nurse Grace's voice say, 'Come in.' She was crouched behind a pile of clean but mixed clothes. She pulled a face at me over them.

'It's a lot,' she said.

I said something inane such as, 'Willing hands make light work.' It sounded so like my mother that it made me blush.

'Yes,' she replied. She stood up and, hitching up the skirt of her uniform, she stepped over the pile, and walked past me to the door and turned the key which she put into her big side pocket.

'Now you're my prisoner,' she laughed.

'I won't be running away.'

'You might, you might.' She gave me that naughty look and ran her hand through her hair.

'Well, what would you like to do?' she asked. I looked over my shoulder at the pile of laundry.

'No,' she said, 'we don't have to start with that yet.' She tipped her head to one side; it reminded me of the dog on the gramophone record.

I giggled. She just continued regarding me. I couldn't think what to do, so I said, 'What would you like to do?'

She smiled. She had a pretty smile. 'Well, if I said I'd like to have my wicked way with you, would you know what I meant?'

I felt my throat go a bit dry. 'No, not exactly, but I'm sure it would be all right,' I heard myself say.

'Can I trust you though, can you keep a secret?' She took her hand out of her pocket and absent-mindedly rubbed the little bump on her forefinger with her thumb. It did look like a wart.

I nodded yes.

'OK. We'll play this game, today it's my choice, I'll choose the rules.'

I just kept looking at her; she was so pretty I kept forgetting to breathe.

'Have you recovered from the operation, appendix, wasn't it?'

'Oh yeah, better a long time ago.' I was thinking about the rules.

'You've got a scar then?'

'Only little.'

'Is it still red?'

'Not really.'

'I think it's manly to have a scar, let's have a look.'

I was suddenly perplexed, caught between the dream girl and the nurse. I guess I didn't move. She stepped towards me and bent to unhitch my snake belt, saying, almost under her breath, 'It's all right, I'm a nurse, remember.'

My trousers and pants slipped down around my ankles and I felt those soft dry hands cup my buttocks for a moment, as though assessing their weight. She then ran one hand across my tummy and followed the line of my scar, which was still rather angry-looking against the rest of my body.

'That's nice.' She screwed up her eyes. 'That's nice too.' She nodded her head at my erect member. 'Does it get like that a lot?' I nodded.

'D'you get the feeling?' She caressed me lightly.

The stress that had caused such frustration became shiveringly wonderful.

'The feeling?'

'Yes, that sweet salty feeling.'

'I did have a feeling shinning up some parallel bars, and it sort of started once when I was climbing a tree, but I had to stop and it – er – went away!'

She laughed. 'I bet it did – no porridge?'

'Porridge?'

'Nothing comes out, squirts out, when you get that feeling?'

'No.'

I thought of an afternoon in a camp we'd built in the Chalk Road debris. Tony Hughes's sister had been the only girl there and an older boy had encouraged us all to show our genitals. The girl had finally shown hers after a lot of cajoling, and when she had left this older guy had rolled about a lot with his hands down his strides. I had asked him what he was doing and he'd said, 'I'm just trying to get the feeling.'

I hadn't really put two and two together.

While these thoughts flashed through my mind, Nurse Grace had removed my clothes, and was massaging parts of my body as it became naked. Taking off my sandals, she said, 'You're going to play dead today; you can only move when I tell you, OK?'

I'd have agreed to anything. She took off her shoes.

'I'm going to teach you about *slow*,' she said as she turned her back to me and raised both my arms around her so that the front of my body was right up close against her back. I could feel the curve of her behind pressing into my groin. I tried to move my hands up to clasp her breasts, but she pulled them down, saying, 'Naughty,' and then, 'Lots of men are hot but I'm going to make you hot and *slow*, so just do what I say.'

She pulled my right hand down over her waspy belt and held it on the mound between her thighs. The excitement! I tried to move my hand against the stiff material. She tapped my finger, the one next to my little finger, 'Just this one, gently with this one.' I did as I was told.

She put her arms backwards around me, clasping her hands on my sacroiliac. 'It's OK to move this,' she said.

I was so thrilled to be fondling her, also trying my best to be gentle and not hurt her. I didn't move for a moment. Then I heard her giggle. 'I'm nicer than the tree, aren't I, rascal?'

She was like that with me; she never let anything get too serious. Even on later occasions, when she arrived without underwear and let me feel her properly. 'Now your touch is right,' she said. That time she made me concentrate on a firm little sliver deep in the soft hair and be doubly gentle. Grace did have abnormally fine pubic hair – I didn't know how rare this was at the time. Then came a moment which seemed to rise out of us both; it was so intense that we both stopped moving. I felt that if I moved a muscle I would faint. As it passed, there was a moment of numbness. I heard Grace murmur something which sounded a bit like, 'Mummy.' As I had been instructed to stay silent once we started playing with each other, I remained mute. But that afternoon, experiencing this incredible togetherness, I said, 'I love you, Grace.'

There was a little pause and Grace moved my left hand and held it.

'This isn't love, rascal, it's just – good!'

She had this way of not letting me get manic, either about us or what we did. It was like a thrilling project we had embarked upon, she teaching, me learning, both enjoying. She was strict, too; everything was within a structure. Outside our afternoons in the laundry, everything went on as normal. Inside more subtle guidelines were kept up. We never talked about ourselves or our lives outside before we'd met. She had a soft accent, which she'd almost lost, which could have been Geordie or Borders, and the only clues I had about her came out of our abstract discussions behind the locked door. One time I confessed that I had felt shy when she first undressed me, and she said that it was normal, being unclothed for the first time by a woman other than one's mother. I said it wasn't that, it was just I hadn't any adult hair yet. I recall her face clouding and she said, rather bitterly I thought, 'It isn't hair that makes a man!' Another time we were, well, resting, I suppose. Grace had brought a Thermos flask with her. She was sitting on the floor against a cupboard. She had drawn her legs up, and her skirt had fallen back over her knees. She had only her white stockings on and, when I thought she was busy pouring into the Thermos cup, I just couldn't resist taking a look up her legs. She caught my eye. I looked away.

'It's all right,' she said, 'I know what boys are like. I like to have myself looked at sometimes.'

I was thinking how different it would be if I had been grown up and, as if reading my thoughts, she said, 'All men are boys,' and after a moment, 'all women are mothers; that's the trouble.'

I looked at her. I suppose she could see from my face that I didn't quite follow her. She handed me the Thermos cup and looked through the steam into my eyes. 'I feel like a guy, I'm just in this body. I suppose that's the real trouble.'

The matron asked me if I would like to stay on an extra week, which I wasn't slow in accepting, and dashed off a postcard home to let them know. A few days later an odd thing happened. I always had this quirk when coming upon somebody I knew not to draw attention to myself but to wait until they had spotted me. It gave me a kick to see that moment when recognition lit up their face. I don't know why. On the Shoeburyness beach one afternoon, to my surprise I saw my mum and dad strolling towards me. As usual I suppressed my impulse to acknowledge them and waited until they saw me. They were not far away and coming straight at me. They both looked right through me and passed me by. I ran down the beach and grabbed them. Dad said, 'Blimey, where did you get that lot?' He was referring to my purple and pink zig-zags. 'You look like Shazam and Son, no wonder we didn't know you.'

He meant Captain or Billy Marvel from the American comics;

he never used anyone's proper name. It turned out that they'd been concerned about my extra week's convalescence and decided to make a day out of the visit. They had brought a whole carrier bag of sweets, but wouldn't tell me where they had come from. Amongst the Liquorice Allsorts and bull's-eyes was a whole slab of fudge. I had never had fudge as good before and I haven't since. It somehow captured in the taste the aromas that drifted out of the Whitefields sweet factory at the Greengate. Many times I'd stood outside after school with my mouth watering and inhaling fit to burst. I badged the magic block in my locker before donating half of my present to matron. I wrapped some up specially for Grace who agreed it was wonderful and thought it might have been made with condensed milk. I looked in the mirror that evening but I looked just the same. I started to get a bit freaked as my day of departure loomed closer, and leaned on Grace to let me go all the way with her. I had this idea that I could somehow bond her to me. She wouldn't have it.

'Why not?' I asked petulantly.

'First of all, it's like opening presents before Christmas, and secondly, this is wonderful now.'

'I really want it to go on. I'll be lost back home without seeing you.'

'Look, you might not understand this at this moment, but I promise it's true. It's difficult for me too, you know. More difficult than you know. One of us has to be strong. Cruel to be kind. And this time it's me.' She looked at me with her lovely velvet eyes. 'If you knew how silly I am, how my head is full of candy floss, you'd soon get tired of me, seeing me, listening to me all the time. What makes it so special now is because it's fragile. Like a big powder-puff rose, at any moment it could just crumble, one heavy touch and nothing, just perfume in the air as the petals fall. Try to not want anything for ever. It spoils things.'

My eyes must have misted up because suddenly she held me close to her and whispered, 'You don't know what life has in store for you.' She laughed. 'My God, the girls, the broken hearts, I can see them all – but don't look back, promise me no looking back.'

'Or I'll turn to salt.'

'Exactly, and you're salty enough as it is.'

When the train pulled out of the station, I knew it was really over. I felt dejected, but tried to look on the bright side. I turned over in my mind all that Grace had told me. I wondered if my life would turn out to be as exciting as she thought. I had my doubts about all the girls, and would they be as pretty as her?

Grace had asked me to stop biting my nails and, as I struggled not to indulge in this comforting habit, I suddenly became aware of her, of her scent. I don't mean perfume, which she didn't wear, but that odour which we all have, peculiar to each of us. Although it was distinct, it was somehow on the edge of my consciousness, so that after smelling my own clothes and not discovering the source, I gave up trying to work it out and consoled myself with the fact that somehow part of her had come with me.

Seven

ENTER ROY CHARLES STUDD

Above: The man himself

Mum was at the ticket barrier at Fenchurch Street. She had left Chris and Richard at Barking Road, so we walked to the shop in Petticoat Lane that sold hot sarsaparilla and had two glasses each before we caught the 40 bus from Aldgate garage. The number 40 was always one of my favourite buses. Exciting things had often been instigated by setting out on its route which symbolised an artery connected to the world up West. Even when we needed a 23 to see Santa at Gamage's, or a 15 for a Lyon's Corner House treat, a 40 always seemed to come along first and if I had my way we got aboard as far as Aldgate.

Mum must have had an inkling of my heartache because she followed when I scooted upstairs to sit in the front seat of the empty bus, and I remember that she went to great pains to point out landmarks of her own youth and places she had taken me to when I was really little. I have never spoken to my mother of any of my philanderings. I suppose the die was cast that afternoon when she was completely open to me and I didn't respond. I can't recall Mum ever offering any advice on the opposite sex except the repeated exchange when she drew my attention to a girl and I invariably scoffed, 'Mum, she's not much to look at,' and she always responded with the same baffling wisdom, 'Perhaps she's got nice ways.'

Mum's big fear was that I would turn out a pansy. It was for this reason that I was never allowed to wear jeans. Apparently, during her evenings as a barmaid at the Abbey Arms she had served a male couple; the extremely feminine one had been encased in a pair of denims and this, combined with a fully made-up face, had given her a shock. What struck me as odd was the ferocious way she put a stop to any of my leanings she found effeminate, but chatting to her sisters she was often in stitches quoting bitchy remarks she'd overheard from customers behind the bar. This paradox extended to cajoling Dad when he called me the queer fella, even though it was plain to me that he was referring to indolence.

The first few days back home were strange. I experienced that sensation of seeing anew things that were very familiar. This was invariably followed by the thought of Grace visiting me and what her opinion would be of my surroundings. I gradually slipped back into routine, even throwing myself into lessons and homework and surprising everyone and myself by coming third in class for the summer term. But there seemed to remain a part of me which had matured, that was now at odds with my boyish activities and attitudes; it gave me flashes of insight into the women I observed and made the girls in my class often seem like a bunch of kittens. I remember these days of my thirteenth year as being lonely and filled with a kind of sadness which I couldn't express or understand other than it felt like home sickness. My nipples became sore and sensitive. A ridge developed under them like a button sewn on back to front. I had my first wet dream, in full technicolour, endlessly entering Hedy Lamarr, and a week later presented myself at Ambrose's, the barber's opposite Bates's Bike Shop, for a trim and shave. Young Mr Ambrose did the honours. Soaping my whole face, accompanied by barber-shop ribaldry, he whipped the bum-fluff from my top lip with just two strokes of his deadly cut-throat, leaving me like a mummy laid out on the chair, my whole face covered in hot towels. I think he wanted me to remember my first shave. Let me assure you, Ambrose, of all the shaves I've had since, including the one from the dwarf on a box looking out across the Ibithincan harbour, the kerbside dervish in Hyderabad and even the octogenarian Mr Brilliant himself at the opening of the Penghaligan perfumery, the Phul-nana treatment I got from you in Barking Road was classic.

Roy Studd must have been shaving for a whole year when I began attaching myself to him, and of all the features which I so envied, his shaded jawline with its circular dimple was the top of my list, closely followed by his jet-black curly hair, triangular eyebrows and, of course, wide grin, which he often spoke through, revealing large white teeth and a generous helping of gums. Try as I did to emulate it, I could never get my lips enough apart to show even a hint of mine. He seemed unaware of his looks, and this was his greatest charm. I was drawn to Roy, subconsciously at first, by his noble manner. He behaved naturally, the way most aristocrats schooled for generations only aspire to behave. I thought by being close to him, perhaps some of his style would rub off on me and I hoped he'd show me a way out; someone as special as him was obviously going places. Of course, I couldn't just present myself at the Court of Studd and announce that I had chosen him to point the way for me. I had somehow to catch his eye and trust he'd welcome me to his group. As has always been my style, when in doubt – observe.

I took to going to Fairbairn alone and watching him from a

distance. Over a year's difference between teenagers can be vast and Roy's sophistication made me acutely aware of this. He was elegant in a way I couldn't imitate for economic reasons. The school uniform my parents were breaking themselves to deck me out in was my only outfit. I had progressed to long trousers – grey flannels, or corduroys which lasted longer – but I was outgrowing threads faster than they could be afforded. One evening on our way to a table-tennis match, me tagging along like a dog, we were waiting for a bus at the Abbey Arms when I caught our reflection from a mirror in Staddon's window: Roy in a sartorial drape and me with patched trousers and last year's blazer halfway up my back. I suddenly didn't know what to do with myself and flushed with inferiority. I had become so accustomed to being the best-dressed boy on the block that I almost hadn't noticed that my two younger brothers, now both at Tolgate, were putting serious limits on the budget for my wardrobe. There seemed to be nothing else I could do but get a job. I approached Mr Brown, who owned the successful sweet, tobacco and paper shop on the corner of Chadwin Road opposite St Cedd's, sweetening the odours of the horse-slaughterer's next door. Mr and Mrs Brown were both middle aged and might have sprung fully grown from the pages of Mabel Lucy Atwell. Mr Brown was habitually sticking his tongue out, and his wife had mottled red legs. Both ate very little lean.

I didn't have much trouble getting the job. How many lunatics wanted to get up at five-thirty into a pitch-black morning? I was handed over to Brian Debell, Teddy's elder blond brother, who was rather staid, and obviously fancied himself as an academic (although he stayed on at Plaistow Grammar until he was almost nineteen before getting the necessary 'A' levels to take him to university). This relationship was the first big hurdle I had to overcome. The second problem was Brian's territory. Either because of his physical maturity or just not being as fly as the other delivery boys, Debell senior had been lumbered with the worst round by a long chalk. The really cushy number, which comprised Chadwin Road itself, then paralleled Selby Road and Brock like the prongs of a fork, was tackled later in the morning by Mr Brown when Mrs Brown arose to mind the shop. The other rounds spread out from the shop like circles in a pond. Our deliveries didn't even start until we had trekked the whole length of Chadwin and Chalk Roads, crossed Prince Regent's Lane, circumvented the Rec. and bypassed West Ham speedway. Our first newspapers made contact with the letter-boxes of Old Beckton Road which ran out of houses and into rubbish strewn open country after about five hundred yards. Some of this terrain featured abandoned Nissen huts and these semi-circular constructions had been turned into squatters' dwellings. We delivered their *Herald*s and *Mirror*s before sweeping directly south of the speedway track to hit a small enclave of houses built in the Thirties, streets hemmed in between the stadium and lido with trim, flower-filled front gardens contrasting with the grime of Canning Town, Custom House and Silvertown.

On the first morning I watched Brian and the other paper-boys make their own piles of newsprint from stacks of papers which filled all three waist-high shelves. Most consulted a hand-written list itemising their streets, house numbers and what went where. Brian, who was apparently an old hand, seemed to know his route by heart. He shuffled his papers neatly together, sometimes sliding one or even two tabloids inside a *Telegraph* or a *Times*, but I groaned when I realised that this great wedge of papers would have to be squeezed into the canvas bag and carried over my shoulder. That first day Brian had me carry the bag the length of Chadwin Road. It felt as though I was carrying a slab of marble. Brian fortified himself with chocolate on the outgoing half when the bag was heaviest; he gave me half his Mars Bar, but it didn't help much. We worked together for a week, then he left and I took over the job. It was murder! The first half was the killer; I soon worked out what few corners could be cut. Leaving the bag at the bottom of those blocks of flats that had stairs, just taking with me the necessary dailies. I would deliver to ten houses and then change shoulders, increasing the number every few days. By the time I had done the long Beckton Road, the bag was reasonably empty and it would be starting to get light. I'd generally get back home by eight o'clock. I kept the bag at home as it saved fifteen minutes at the end of the day.

Dad had often said, 'Don't start anything you can't finish,' and I repeated this motto to myself as I slogged through those first weeks, having serious doubts about my entry into working life. My first week's wages totalled 12/6d – a ten-shilling note and half a crown. I was pleased as Punch. I asked Mum if I should contribute any to costs at home, but she said there was plenty of time for that. So I put ten shillings away and spent the half crown. Half a pound of cherries and *Against All Flags* in the front row of the circle at the Boleyn Odeon.

Observing Roy was both exhilarating and crushing. It turned out that he was one of those guys who was just good at everything. Week nights were taken up with billiards, snooker, darts and table-tennis; at weekends he played football in the winter and cricket for the first eleven in the summer. One night we passed on the stairs and he acknowledged me, saying something that sounded like, 'Whoop – John.'

I was taken aback and, not understanding the Cockney oldspeak, replied blankly, 'Wot?'

He just grinned and didn't stop to explain. I couldn't believe I'd blown it. There were so many things I wanted to talk to him about. There were a lot of legends surrounding Roy. One story current at the time concerned a girl called Kay Reid, who was so smitten with him that she climbed the very high wall of the bombed Odeon opposite Star Lane and threatened to throw herself off unless Roy came and reassured her of his feelings. Roy interrupted his dinner at his home in the neighbouring Braemar Road to come and reassure her. It is hard to know what, if any, was the substance of these kinds of stories. I certainly never became intimate enough, or knew of anyone who was close enough, to confront Roy himself. I believed all the tales that added glamour to my hero, and anyway a court wouldn't be a court without intrigue.

Shortly after our first exchange, I was again hanging around the first-floor table-tennis room. There was quite a crowd waiting to play on both tables, and it was a 'winner stays on' situation. Roy had been on one table for a few consecutive games and, while he was playing Terry Harris, one of the three full-size snooker tables in the adjoining room became vacant and a group of boys opted for that. So when Terry, also a first-team member, beat Roy, I was the only spectator in the room. Roy congratulated his opponent and turned to me with a grin which showed the slightly serrated edges of his front teeth. He offered me the bat he'd been using and said, 'Wanna game?'

I gulped.

'Sure.'

I took the bat which was still warm and went up to the full-size Jacques table. Roy went over to the leaded windows which looked out over Barking Road and hitched a hip on to the low radiator. He

said to Terry (Harris, as I later discovered) as we knocked up,
'Watch him, he's a leftie.'

I half turned towards him, and he sort of scrunched his bottom
lip up, flattening out his dimple. I felt he was giving me the OK to
avenge his defeat. I wasn't anywhere near the standard of my
opponent but I played as if my life depended on it and got to deuce
before being beaten. Roy reclaimed his bat and said, 'You play well,
you should practise a bit, get a backhand smash.'

He demonstrated his action, dropping his left shoulder and
leaning away from where he would be sending the ball.

'Yeah, I will.'

'OK. See you around.'

'Yeah, say that's a neat shirt!' I said, wanting to prolong the
moment.

'It's a Dino special,' he said, stroking the rolled collar.

'Dino special?' I said, thinking it was the brand of shirt.

'Like what Dean Martin always wears; this is not the real thing.'
He considered for a moment. 'If I could get hold of a real one,
wow, wouldn't that be something – this is the nearest I could get,
it's a Dayton roll-collar, they flog them at Christies.'

He named a man's shop at Trinity Church; it was right by the
corner bus stop for the 106 and 175 and sold American and
American-style clothes. I must have looked in that window a
hundred times but had never been inside. The truth was that it
hadn't occurred to me, firstly because it was a man's shop and
didn't cater for boys, and secondly because the styles and prices
were too outrageous for me even to consider. Well, Roy had
shopped there and so could I. The next weekend I gave Saturday
morning pictures a miss and took the 106 to Trinity Church. By
nine-thirty I was standing outside the shop looking up at the
painted decal on the front: crossed Union Jack and the Stars and
Stripes. Christies! A loud bell clanked as I put my weight against
the door. Behind the glass case which doubled as a counter, a man
with a crew-cut and rimless spectacles was serving a customer. I
nosed around. The shop had a different odour from the other
clothes shops I knew, the mixture of materials smelt different. No
attempt at made-to-measure here. Racks of jackets and self-
supporting trousers, bird's-eyes, diagonals, broken diagonals and
window-pane checks in outlandish colours. Powder-blues and
apple-greens fought for my gaze; it was Hank Jansen in techni-

colour. Clutching a slim jim, the other customer left, and the rimless glasses turned their attention to me.

I took a deep breath. 'I'm looking for a Dayton roll. I wonder if you have my size?'

'What size is that, man?' He lowered his face to look at me over his glasses. The top of his head showed through the fine hair. It reminded me of my efforts to grow a lawn at the back of 124 with seed I'd cadged from the groundsman of the Rec.

'I'm not sure,' I said, feeling stupid. 'I've put on weight.'

'In that case, buddy, we have to measure you up.' He slipped his signeted ring-hand into his trouser pocket and produced a small tape measure. I thought for a moment it was from a Christmas cracker, with predictions on the back. He eased it expertly round my pale scrawny neck. I held my breath. 'Yup.' I smelt spearmint and I bet it was the long uncoated strips that girls who went out with Yanks chewed during the War.

'OK, let's have a look at the arm-length.'

He stretched out my arm and ran the tape along it.

'Hey, that's a long arm; you're gonna be a tall fella.'

He went back behind the counter, opened a drawer about face height and whipped out two packed shirts.

'Blue or white?'

I looked at the sought-after items; my hand clutched the four brick-red notes in my pocket – don't walk in unless you can walk out.

'How much are they?'

'Thirty-five and six . . . thirty-five to you, sir.'

'Blue, I'll take the blue.'

'Anything else?'

The four weeks' wages were already on the counter. 'Not today,' I replied weakly.

The label on the collar said, 'DAYTON – SANFORISED. IRON WHEN DAMP.'

My efforts to look like one of the chaps were seriously curtailed when I was fired by Mr Brown. Just when everything had seemed tickerteeboo. Having survived the nightmare initiation, I had progressed to the Cumberland Road round, much more up-market, lots of *Times* and *Telegraph*s, even deliveries of *Motor* and *Harper's Bazaar*. Of course, there were the wealthier eccentricities to be coped with: 'Please get the new boy to push the papers right

through the letter-box. It made such a dreadful draught yesterday,'
and four doors along, 'Can't the papers be left in the letter-box?
The awful bump woke me clean up.' I gritted my teeth and
weathered all that, and was even trusted to go out collecting the
money on Saturdays with a shoulder cash-bag and expenses for a
snack of tea and tomatoes on toast at May's Café, perhaps even
catching a glimpse of Lesley Garner, the owner's daughter, who
sometimes helped out at weekends. She was at Sara Bonnells
School for Girls and looked fetching in her green and cream
uniform, with a personal scent I always associated with prosperity, a
mixture of cooking oil and soap; expensive, not Lifebuoy like we
used.

On the fateful Thursday I had slipped out of school at the break
and, not wanting to arouse Mum's suspicions by getting home too
early, I nipped into Brown's for a chocolate honeycomb bar. I was
almost out of the door when Mrs Brown, whose motto was 'If you
want anything done, get somebody else to do it', asked me if I
wouldn't mind numbering the afternoon papers that customers
collected from the shop: 'Just leave them there on the shelf –
displayed so they are easy to see.'

She lifted up the counter flap and waddled through into the
living-room. I watched the mottled legs and feet in furry carpet
slippers disappear. Then I heard the low armchair groan as she sat
into it, and the opening line of 'Are you sitting comfortably?' from
Listen with Mother. I mentally noted three-thirty. I was into
calligraphy at the time, ageing paper by first staining it with tea and
scorching the edges to make it resemble parchment, then drawing
on the characters. I had memorised the whole alphabet and
numerals of Old English Script and practised them whenever I
could so as not to forget the shapes. That is exactly what I did on
the afternoon editions. I may have overdone it a bit in trying to
make the HB pencil lead look like Indian black, but was at a loss to
fathom the furor that followed.

Mr Brown made a special trip to our house to tell Mum 'he
could no longer see his way clear to keeping me employed' and
Mum kept wringing those sad, chapped hands with the nail
missing, her cheeks and neck flushed, saying, 'Oh, Terry, why did
you do it, why? It was such a good job, you were getting on so well.'

I didn't have any answer. I'd have given myself eight out of ten
considering the quality of the paper, but it did strike me as ironic

that other kids had been robbing them blind, snatching fistfuls of chocolate over the counter when their backs were turned and indulging in a complex system of lightening the weekly collection bag. I was definitely in the minority of employees who did the job and took only the wages. Mum stopped our papers and I never went into the shop again. Although I heard that just before Mum and Dad left the area for good, Mum gave Mrs Brown a right mouthful about the real goings on of more helpful helpfuls.

Eight

ELECTRIC FEET

Above: What can I say? The lovely Barbara.

Electric Feet

When I was accepted by Roy and his chums, albeit as a kind of mascot, I was in my element. Working life had netted me the shirt, a knitted silk tie and a pair of black slip-on shoes, from the private house on the corner of James Street and New Barn Street. Mum said the boxes of shoes that filled the living-room 'probably fell off a lorry'. I had earmarked my next six months' salary for a light grey window-pane check, but I was still making do with my bum-freezer blazer and was very conscious that I stood out from the others. The first time I went to an away table-tennis match in a church hall opposite the roller-skating rink at Forest Gate, I was taken aback by its being a mixed club and actually saw for the first time how girls reacted to Roy's presence. In one way it confirmed my feeling that he was special and the prestige of being in the retinue transferred itself to me; at the same time I felt even more insignificant, just one of many onlookers. Roy played well that night, oblivious to the female attention, but from comments on the bus home, nothing much had escaped him. We would often leave the bus at the same stop, and I would pause a moment and watch him stroll away, his holdall hanging from the tips of his fingers, his body illuminated by the lights from the Abbey Arms and the public convenience, the latter with its girder arcs and cut-out sign lit within like a Chinese lantern proclaiming GENTS. Then there would settle over me a loneliness and to cheer myself up I would do the sideways run I had invented, all the time pondering how he must feel, how it would be to be like that, just like that.

With Roy's friends I became quite relaxed but this ease never extended to Roy himself because I was so in awe of him. Yet he was certainly easy-going enough. When the club was closed for a few weeks, I felt such a sense of loss that I wandered about the area where he lived, hoping to come across him, but it never even crossed my mind just to go and knock on his door and see if he was in. None of these feelings struck me as odd. I figured if other boys had these crazes, they kept quiet about them the same as me. This crush was completely non-sexual; it was so innocent that I call it only a crush now, then I didn't define it at all. Sexual thoughts were reserved for Grace. In my heart of hearts I knew I would never see her again and as the months passed, my memories, even the most passionate ones, became dreamlike. I was having a harder and harder time coping with my growing sexuality and despaired of ever being touched by love again.

Boys graduated from Fairbairn House when they were fourteen and every year one boy in his last year was elected captain. It was a great honour, his name was engraved on the silver cup and also painted on the board in the Sunday Assembly Room. Although my attendance at Fairbairn was totally without distinction, I set my heart on getting this honour. I entered club competitions and submitted several paintings along with my school chum, Willy Cook, for an exhibition held in the Front Hall. The power of Fairbairn House was embodied in the person of Sir Ian Horobin, the warden. He was the Conservative MP for some constituency or other, Oldham perhaps, and kept an apartment in a block of flats which adjoined the back of the club, with a front entrance on Avenons Road. Sir Ian, or Spike as we called him – a nickname he was given for allegedly overseeing the goings on in the communal bath area perched on a shooting-stick – was an imposing, even frightening figure. He always made me nervous anyway, partly because his dress was archaic; his stiff detachable collars, his closely cropped hair, a pince-nez perched on his beaky nose, held in place by what appeared to be little gold screws, set him apart. Added to this, he had an explosive temper, similar to Mr Priest's, the PT teacher at school.

There were all kinds of gossip about Sir Ian, the strongest being that he was a bit of a 'ginger beer'. I didn't really subscribe to this as there was really nothing cissy about him at all. Some evenings he would prowl about the club ordering boys to pick up cigarette ends and generally making a wet blanket of himself (he raised his voice to other staff more than he did to us). I just kept out of his way for the most part. So it came as a bit of a surprise when one evening he congratulated me upon my paintings and invited me to bring any others I might have for him to look at.

'Shall we say Saturday afternoon at the residence?'

I was rather chuffed by this request and spent the week collecting my stuff together and making a cardboard folder, so as to present it in an artistic manner. On Saturday at three o'clock I rang the doorbell and Mrs Scott, the housekeeper, showed me up into his quarters. It was extremely grand and in complete contrast to the scruffy back street it looked out upon. What impressed me most was the size of the room: it was bigger than the whole of our downstairs put together. It had subtly defined areas: two chairs faced each other across a silk rug, and beside the unwindowed wall was a bed without sheets and blankets just covered in biscuit-beige velvet with a matching cushion. In the middle of the room were an ottoman and an austere but elegant small table upon which Sir Ian placed my folder. He pulled the heavy curtains across one of the four windows which overlooked the street, saying, 'We shouldn't look at them in direct sunlight.'

I opened my folder and he came and stood close to me, first looking over my shoulder, and then leaning over me turning the paintings, resting his hand on my back. I could feel the hair on my neck standing up and I smelt the aftershave he was wearing as his face angled close to mine. It smelt how I imagined oriental scents would smell. He slipped his hand lightly on to my neck. It must have goosepimpled. I was too scared to move. His other hand reached around me and rubbed the outside of my trousers. In spite of myself I was getting a hard on. He moved behind me.

'Yes,' he was saying, his head close to the back of mine. I could feel his breath. 'That's a nice rod, a very nice rod.'

I felt him pressing himself against me, almost bending me over the table, his breathing becoming heavier. I was really petrified. I found myself looking at the illustrated blue tiles around the fireplace and then suddenly Grace flashed into mind. I remembered how firm she had been with me. I made a grab at his hand, pulled it away from me and edged along the table. I heard myself say, 'I've got to make a move now.'

I moved instinctively towards the light section of the room. I heard him shuffling my paintings together, walking across the carpet towards me. I turned and took the folder without looking. He said, 'You won't lag on me, will you?'

I'd never heard that expression before. I just nodded. He pushed something into my top pocket; it was a ten-shilling note. I reached for it, intending to give it back, but he stopped my hand.

'No, no, keep it, I want you to have it.' He smiled. 'Pocket money.'

I had never seen him smile before. It didn't suit him. I just made for the door, and as I left I heard him say again, 'You won't lag on me?'

I walked left towards Denmark Street. I was in a kind of shock; so that's what it was all about, what Ethel was so worried about. What I had been so keen to do to Grace, he had wanted to do to me. How different it was. On the corner there was a sweet shop that was my all-time favourite, Bel's, opposite Denmark Street School. They sold drinks, homemade from sherbet, by the glass and ice lollies. Boy smokers bought packs of five Woodbine filtertips, the cheapest, there. Feeling punchy, I was making for the welcoming steps of that shop, when someone called, 'Oi Tel, wotcha!'

It was Teddy Debell bowling along on the other side of the street. 'You all right? You look a bit Tom and Dick.'

In a whisper I spilled out what had just happened. Teddy's big eyes became bigger like saucers, but his response was funny.

'He gave you half a nicker?'

'Yeah, tried to give it him back but . . . '

'So you got it then?'

'Yeah.' I pulled the offending note out of my top pocket like a handkerchief.

'Cripes, d'you think he'll give me one?'

'Listen, Ted – he's you know, after yer ring!'

'Oh, don't worry about that. Listen, you hang about here and I'll just see if I can get ten bob as well, we'll nip off to the pictures!'

He trotted off, whistling. I felt dizzy. I sat on the steps of the sweet shop. A few minutes later he was back.

'Haw, the old nanny said he was resting, still we got ten bob, where shall we go?'

I had to laugh; trust old Ted to put things in perspective. My first encounter of the second kind.

Sexuality always struck me as odd, or rather I had always been intrigued by its different manifestations. The hornier I felt – an almost continuous condition during the years at high school – the more shy and withdrawn I became in the presence of the opposite sex, even after I knew some girls quite approved. This contradiction fascinated me and I suppose I've always had a soft spot for women who reflected this ambivalence. Trying to think back to the point when this seed was sown, the name of Dimsie comes to mind.

I was all of eight when she came into my life. My mother must have despaired of my ever learning to read. When I finally did, just two years before the greatly feared eleven-plus, she was so relieved and delighted that I was instantly showered with books from the Beckton Road Library. I was too raw to know how to find books of interest off my own bat, so Mum took it upon herself. The books she selected for me were those she had read and loved when she too was young. And so my relationship with Dimsie began. My mother's decision to expose her newly literate son to the heroine of a girl's boarding-school saga should not be misinterpreted. The very first literature, if it may be so termed, to pierce the miasma of my schoolboy indolence had been her yearly gift of Alfred Bestall's immortal *Adventures of Rupert Bear*. Although the rhyming couplets which appeared under Bestall's extraordinary and evocative line drawings were not his own work, the illustrations were so wondrous, so suggestive of a barely reachable magic, that I struggled to master those lines of doggerel with a fervour notably absent from my half-hearted endeavours at Tolgate Road Primary. Thus my first efforts to read and comprehend the language of Milton and Shakespeare were fuelled by my determination to understand the mind and imagination of an artist of genius and inventor of a bear. From Rupert I graduated to Gypsy Petulengro in my mother's copy of *Woman's Own*. It was probably seeing me poring over my stars in *Woman's Own* and trying to grasp what great events Fate held in store for me that gave Ethel the idea of introducing me to Dimsie and her endless adventures. I did not 'identify' with Dimsie quite as Ethel and other addicts of Dorita Fairlie Bruce's creation must have done. I didn't even want to go to boarding-school except perhaps to peel off Dimsie's uniform and share her dormitory cot for a night or two. Yet it must be confessed, Dimsie was the first female, real or imaginary, of whom I desired knowledge in the biblical sense. Even before I gave my longing heart to Gene Tierney and Hedy Lamarr, it was Dimsie's fetching combination of chestnut curls and leggy middle-class refinement which hit me where it hurt, setting the pattern and quest for the English rose with the hidden quality of wantonness which has wreaked havoc in so many manly hearts, including my own.

When Dimsie grew up to become a herbalist, healing scars with oil of marigold and so on, it became clear to me then that she was never about to unlock her passionate nature. She lost me there. I preferred her when she wore indecorously short skirts and seemed to promise rapture. I went on to the hair-on-chest library school of Biggles and Dick Barton and didn't think of Dimsie much after that. But judging by the mass appreciation of the style of Princess Di, the mould and matrix is intact and not confined to me. Mum could not have known what she was letting me in for, but she didn't do badly all things considered.

The automatic reaction in a physical situation was what I found unnerving, as if my peter had a life of its own, or was aroused by conditions the rest of me was unaware of. Take my little episode with Horobin. By no stretch of the imagination would he have qualified as fanciable, even with his dousing of Eau de Kananga, and yet part of me had responded as if I'd been in the golden clasp of Rita Hayworth. I was preoccupied enough to ask questions on this topic in biology class, although the giggles from Barbara Say, Jean Appleton and other girls already wearing bras foreshortened the Aristotelian line of questioning I had in mind. But I did glean that certain animals gave off a particular odour when in season, which caused a contagious excitement. It occurred to me that perhaps we had lost this sense, and I spent weeks trying to redevelop it by unobtrusively sniffing girls I liked until some prat of a French mistress caught me in the act, drew everyone's attention to me and made me stand outside the class for the whole period.

In the summer of '52 I went off to what was to be my last summer camp with Fairbairn House. The club had been donated a large field within walking distance of the sea at Sandwich in Kent. All of us city hounds lived under canvas for a fortnight, out of reach of the Norman town of Sandwich itself with its quaint streets and genteel inhabitants. Visits to town were strictly meted out, one tent at a time. As tents were made up of eleven boys, there were inter-tent competitions of every eleven-a-side game imaginable, with cash prizes. This was my third camp and I was captain of a tent which I had politically put together to contain my best chums who were also dab hands at sport: Colin Cavanagh, Johnny Tanner and Teddy Debell to name but a few, and even a court jester with the wonderful name of Raymond Wacker. We won everything, scooping up enough prize money on the final day to buy presents for family at home. On the last morning Colin Stevens cut his hand with the bread-cutting machine. That summer we came home in a charabanc which turned us out beside the club. We must have looked like the Three Musketeers, Teddy, Colin and I, walking down Chadwin Road all brown as nuts, Colin with his arm in a sling and all in our going-away suits which had been stashed in our kitbags and used as pillows since the morning we arrived. Mum, waiting at our street door, had a moment of panic. Thinking that her eldest son was swathed in bandages, she had overlooked the lanky stranger with his new suit trousers parting company with his shoes by at least three inches. I was on my way to my six-foot target; my visualisation programme was working.

About three months later I started getting such pain in my feet that it took me about five minutes to get out of bed and put weight on them. Of course at first Tom and Ethel assumed that I was malingering, but eventually I was dragged off to Dr Brandreth's spartan green surgery and forwarded from there to a Gothic hospital in Poplar. All our family hated St Andrew's because so many of our relations had died there. I wasn't aware of this, but it was a harrowing place and always reminded me of the opening of *Oliver Twist*. The Department of Physical Medicine was on the ground floor. The first time, Mum and I went by tube to Bromley Station, where nobody ever seemed to get on or off, but when it was determined that I needed treatment every day, I went straight after school on my Hercules roadster. It was a long haul, whichever route I took. I finally settled for going over the Silvertown Bridge to the Blackwall Tunnel, turning right at Poplar Hospital (where the last black rat in England was traced) and continuing all the way down Brunswick Road to Bromley by Bow where the hospital rose up out of a hinterland of bomb-damaged wasteland. The physio had explained to Ethel that my speedy gain in height had thrown strain upon the set of my foot.

'Rather like what happens to a woman when she wears stiletto heels regularly,' he said, glancing with a certain amount of approval at Mum's small heels.

'We had a girl in here last week whose body was so out of alignment she was sticking her chin out like a chicken!' His eyes swivelled to me. 'That's what's happened to you, in a smaller way.'

'I've been doing this technique for urging . . . '

Mum stopped me with a look.

'What were you saying, doctor?' she asked.

The man sat me on a chair and made me lift the toes of my left foot and the heel of my right and then simultaneously switch positions. 'Do that every morning for a few minutes,' he said, after making sure I could do it correctly. He then took me into another room full of machinery where he put my feet into separate little baths which had water just covering the bottom. A zinc plate was put under each foot and connected by a wire to a machine with knobs on. He switched on and turned a knob until I felt an electric shock as both feet lifted up out of the water as if on strings. I sat watching my feet go up and down for ten minutes before I was dried off and sent to rejoin Mum.

When we were out of the hospital Mum said, 'I wish you'd keep your ideas to yourself, or at least not talk about it when we're out.'

'He agreed with me; he said it was like wearing high heels.'

'He said because you shot up,' she cut in. 'He didn't say you'd done it.'

'Well, it happened, it happened to me. Energy follows thought,' I said, quoting a *Health and Efficiency* magazine I'd ogled in the second-hand book mart at Greengate.

Mum gave me one of those fatigued looks that I'd grown to recognise as 'How did it happen to me?' She said, 'Just talk about things like that indoors.'

I reported at the hospital every afternoon. The Department of Physical Medicine was so full of misshapen people that most days I got out the foot baths, hooked myself up, gave myself ten minutes of shocks and left unnoticed. This went on for about a month before I was discharged. It was really tedious on top of homework. But my tedious foot treatment turned out to be more useful than I could have dreamed.

That year I was in a school play. Although it was only a minor part, I did get to wear a cavalier wig and try my hand at make-up using my own Leichner 5 and 9. I still have the José Florez make-up box with what remains of my greasepaint collection. Those odorous sticks, their four-stringed lyre trademark, with tint spelt TEINT, and the address, Acre Lane, London SW2. I don't even know if L. Leichner is still in business, but those tools of my trade have been with me for over thirty years; they are still in the working order they were in that night in the assembly hall when I got to tread the boards for the first time in a play directed by Miss Wilks, the English mistress with the National Health specs, who didn't approve of my glamorous début and slammed on an extra layer of 6 and 8A so hard that it made my skin smart. The smell as I open the box transports me instantly to the geography room behind the stage, festooned with wigs, costumes and half-dressed would-be players. Kipling was right to say forget sight and sound: it is *smell* that makes the heart strings crack.

I was made captain of Fairbairn. I had assumed my rejection of the warden would have put the lid on that, but perhaps he was nervous that I'd spill the beans, or maybe there just weren't as many contenders as I'd imagined. The cup which endorsed my appointment, that cup which I so wanted Ethel to have, took the whole year to be engraved and we didn't even see it, let alone have it on the sideboard, between the cut-glass fruit bowls where I'd envisaged it. Of course, Mum was terrifically pleased and I felt at last that something was happening which would fulfil her hopes and my ambitions, although I didn't really have a clear picture what they were.

Nine

BLUE TANGO

Above: Brian Cosgrove, Bernie Wilson, Ken Jude
and yours truly with the French team

Ethel Proud entered my life in October '52. In the late Forties and early Fifties when Rab Butler's scheme to educate the masses was beginning to pay off, somebody had the bright idea of taking a second look at those students who had failed the eleven-plus when they were fourteen; this was to give possible late developers another chance. A special class of these second-netted bright sparks was incorporated into Plaistow Grammar; it was known as Lower Five T. Most of these denizens of LVT were late of secondary modern schools where the going was a lot less genteel than the rarefied atmosphere we enjoyed. Long sideburns and bootlace ties began appearing in the corridors, until Mr Barwise, the headmaster, put his foot down and insisted on school uniform being worn. The new boys were mostly tough. I actually saw one of them retaliate against Mr Priest's bullying, which was exactly what the gym teacher wanted and he knocked the boy senseless, but the fact that he actually took on a teacher was both shocking and thrilling. Although I didn't have the courage to try myself, I felt the contagious wave of violence sweep across me and I held myself tense waiting to see if any of the other boys would jump this object of hatred. I know I would have joined them. Nobody did. I looked at the crêpe-soled creepers of the boy on the ground. He was lying just in front of the boys' entrance. His body was twitching and lumps were coming up on his face, his trousers had rucked up as he had fallen and his white socks covering thin ankles which would normally have looked flash just looked sad.

The classrooms at school had windows on both sides and the inner one looked across the corridors on to the grass quadrangles. Anyone using the corridor during lesson-time therefore had a good view of what was happening inside. I often used to get excused to go to the lavatory, more often than not to breathe the fresh air and break the boredom. Once outside my own classroom, I felt a barely perceptible shift as though my presence had dimmed. I walked stealthily by, viewing the swotting inmates who were unaware of being watched. As I passed the new LVT classroom, I slowed my steps to get a better look at the new arrivals. Gerrard Ward was teaching; he had obviously set the class work and was hunched over a book on his table out front. His pupils were all scratching away, now and then mechanically dipping a pen into a sunken inkwell. But in the middle of the group was a girl who wasn't bent over her paper, she wasn't pausing for thought either; she was just sitting, unnoticed, staring into space in a world of her own. I paused to get a better look at her: in profile she looked a bit like Grace, the same delicate nose, fine blonde hair, but when she turned her face towards me, as if my attention had intruded on her reverie, the resemblance vanished. I moved on, out of range of that still look. It had touched me though; her features hung in my mind. I began to look out for her. The school and surrounding streets became a frame of reference for the occasions I glimpsed her. In the domestic science corridor with a dab of flour on her pencil skirt. Outside the gym, her forehead moist. I always thought of her skin colour as saffron. It wasn't, but it's what I imagined saffron to be like before I saw any. I didn't even know her name until Warren Hopps, Warren with the Burt Lancaster hair and easy manner, told me she was called Ethel Proud, but only responded to Toni.

In the same breath he said that she was going out with Terry Curtis from LVA. I could hardly believe it. The three weeks' extension to the summer break provided by the family hop-picking ritual which I'd accepted so gleefully had finally rebounded on me. I decided I'd better get some griff on my rival.

There was a definite snobbism based on the category of which form one was in. The A and B forms had Latin and German, and we had woodwork and domestic science. Although these were the only variations on the timetable, nobody was taken in; we were second best and that was that. Worse still, there were some amazing looking dudes in the A form, and I had the sinking feeling it was one of them who had hold of my dream girl. As it turned out, the two main Lotharios were friends: Terry Curtis and Micky Lake. Lake was the better looking of the two in my opinion. He was tall, with thick dark-brown hair, straight like Cary Grant's. He had an elegance like Cary as well; you could see him doing justice to a white tie and tails. But his mate, Terry, did have great hair, I had to give him that. It was black and curly and softened the square set of his features. His head was too large to be really handsome. He was short and his legs bowed a bit, giving him the rolling gait of a sailor. But he had a presence that was hard not to acknowledge. I've always been interested in the kind of guys that women choose. You can tell a lot about a woman by her book. Probably this pastime started with my naïve observation of Toni and Terry.

I had never had a girlfriend. Grace was the first female that had taken an interest in me. It didn't worry me particularly. I had all sorts of fantasies about sirens I'd seen at the movies, and assumed that a Gene Tierney would walk into my life when the time was right. I had no way of knowing how I would make out with a girl. Grace had said to me, 'It's the girls who do the choosing, men think they do but we know better. It makes me chuckle when fellas do their heavy come on. You let the ladies make the move, Master Terence, you will save yourself a lot of effort and you won't make a fool of yourself.'

I tried to follow her advice, but the feelings erupting inside me made me unsure.

One evening I was cutting home from the Boleyn down Boundary Road, intending to walk over the dumps while the sun was setting. The dumps were old slag heaps that were a permanent feature of our landscape. Nothing grew on them but sometimes little fires still broke out which, with the gassy odours and the ruined 'haunted hospital' that bordered them on the furthest corner, made them an unsavoury habitat for everyone except desperate lovers and us kids, who had slid down their slopes on discarded metal trays and bits of corrugated iron. I always found these barren mounds welcoming, even romantic, and often explored them on my own, especially after Dad found there a whole box of glass eyes of different colours which could be held over the eye like a very startling monocle. That evening, at the Boundary Road entrance two figures were coming towards me on the other side of the road: Terry Curtis and Toni. I slowed down and they turned left towards the street where she lived. For the first time I noticed the rather uneven rhythm of her walk, maybe caused by her tight skirt, which gave her a certain vulnerability as though she were not sure of her contact with the ground. Terry had his right arm possessively around her shoulder and was squeezing her to him. She was wearing a red sweater which couldn't have been described as loose. It was the first time I'd seen her out of uniform. She was much more developed than the other girls in my year.

It was also the first time I'd felt adult jealousy. It stopped me dead. All kinds of pictures reeled through my head; after all they were leaving a known trysting spot. I saw him stroking her smooth sallow face, looking into those cloudy blue eyes, fondling her grown-up body, and I remembered a couple I'd seen years before on these same dumps, a girl on her back with skirt hitched up and white legs astride, and between them a guy lying fully dressed. The image whipped me as I compelled myself to keep walking. I began not to sleep well for the first time since the pre-scholarship days.

From the day we'd moved to 124, Chris and I had slept in the front room. I had never liked the back bedroom in our house and felt deprived when Richard was old enough to sleep on his own and Mum and Dad swapped us over. There was no logic attached to my resentment: the room was bigger and looked out across the best garden around, off limits to us except for viewing. I tried not to look at it too much, as its unused spaciousness – heavily laden pear trees, Conferences left to rot in the autumn, virgin snow drifts in the winter – always filled me with bitterness every time I contemplated this forbidden pleasure garden. In all the years I lived at 124 I never set eyes on our wealthy neighbours, whose fruit dropped unnoticed by its owners within feet of our fence. These wooden planks finally disintegrated after I'd left home, when only a piece of string marked the boundary. Even then Ethel wouldn't allow us to trespass or scrump the fruit, but we heard from the occupants soon enough when the carpenter mistakenly resurrected the fence six inches in our favour.

I had always enjoyed looking out on to the street from the front bedroom, and our old room housed a dressing table and wardrobe with a mirrored door which was part of a suite that had been the first thing purchased by Tom and Ethel when they married. They'd since acquired more deluxe models, which stayed in the back room when the sleeping quarters were rearranged. Our wardrobe never held much – my threadbare collection of ties on a string across the door was the only real constant – but the fact that it stayed in what was now my parents' bedroom and their clothes remained in ours diluted my sense of having a space of my own. The front room definitely had a nicer feel and was full of warm associations from the dark outlines made every year by our presents at the foot of the faded red eiderdown early on Christmas mornings.

Our only sister arrived on 23 December in '51. Later Dad erected a plasterboard partition against the far wall of our bedroom, slicing off enough of the room to house a small bed for the newly christened Lynette Mary. That Christmas was made all the more special by this arrival. Mum had decided to have her fourth child at home, and the barren arctic front room was temporarily transformed into a cosy maternity ward, with a constant roaring coal fire and the double bed brought downstairs for the occasion. I thought it a wonderful start in life for our sister to be born at home and we all crowded around the bed seconds after she arrived. Mum was so happy with the little longed-for package she imagined would become her companion and friend in life the way she had been to her mother. It didn't turn out like that, but for a year our house was filled with the gentle aroma of mother's milk and her lullabies. Mum refused to have any of us immunised. We were seldom ill but then she had old-fashioned ideas and breast-fed us for as long as possible. The newly divided back room scarcely held Chris and Richard's double bed, let alone my narrow single nearest the door, and at night I would lie awake on my side, alternately looking at the cold bare grate and the rag rug on the floor which Mum and I had made during the Blitz. Long nights thinking of Toni and listening to the varying rhythms of my brothers' breathing.

One afternoon I saw her coming along from the girls' exit at the fire station end of school. She was with her friend whom my police work had divulged as Maureen Holloway, a redhead, well ginger actually. They were sharing a bag of cherries. Maureen was giggling and making a fuss of spitting out the stones. She saw me and nudged Toni as they came towards the bus stop. Toni and I looked at each other and her expression changed. She didn't smile but her face softened, almost as though she knew and understood.

Maureen said, 'Give him a cherry,' to Toni and to me, 'Would you like one?'

I nodded at her and took a couple, placing them over my ear.

Maureen giggled. 'What's your name then?'

'Terry,' I said, 'Terry Stamp.'

'Oooh! Another Terry.' She nudged Toni again.

'Yeah,' I said, 'the name's becoming as common as mud!'

'I wouldn't say that.' Toni spoke for the first time with almost no volume. Her voice was broken husky like a young man's; it was in keeping with her walk.

I waited for her to speak again but she didn't. I heard Maureen say cheerfully, 'Wonderful day, great to be alive, ain't it?'

'I wouldn't go that far,' I said. It was a remark I'd heard my dad make once in response to the same question. The expression in Toni's eyes changed but she smiled.

Maureen took her friend's arm as though to imply that was 'enough for today', saying, 'Oooh, he's a live one all right.'

It was awful; the more I saw her the worse I felt. It was like after

I'd left the convalescent home but all the time. I'd heard that falling in love was like seeing the Almighty's face. If this was it, it was an even bigger disappointment than smoking. Maureen Holloway, however, turned out to be a helpful ally and soon made it clear that she was on my case; either because she didn't like Toni's present boyfriend, or the idea of having one serious beau; more probably she just fancied my chum Teddy who although still in the fourth form was quite a hunk. Several foursomes took place, Maureen acting as a go-between, enabling me to keep a low profile. Our first outing was to a fair in Barking Park, where we went on as many of the scary rides as we could afford and then Teddy won us all coconuts at the darts stall. Excitement was a good diversion since Toni and I didn't have much to say to each other. I think her manner was just quiet, sort of introverted, at odds with how she looked. I was plain speechless most of the time. One problem was not being able to adjust the arrangement of my uncircumcised private parts which became unbearably sensitive in close proximity to Toni, and being second string to Terry Curtis was another. At the end of this evening Teddy took Maureen home to Winkfield Road, just past the bus garage off Greengate Street, and I walked Toni to Kingsland Road. It was one of the better streets; most houses had an area, 'arie' we pronounced it, and a proper privet hedge in front. When we arrived at Number 36, she opened her gate and turned to face me. I smelt the distinct perfume of chrysanthemums which wafted between us.

'Goodnight then,' came the gruff voice.

'Did you have a good time?' I passed her one of the two coconuts I was holding; the milk swashed about inside. I moved my hand, intending to hold her arm, but she turned slightly, saying, 'Yes, thank . . . ' when the back of my hand brushed her breast. Neither of us spoke; I put my hand in my pocket.

She turned to go and at her door she said, 'See you Monday.'

'Monday?'

'At school.'

'Yeah – goodnight.'

I met up with Teddy at the late-night tea stand which parked at Greengate, next to the public convenience island. He was leaning against the high counter with his foot between the spokes of the wheel, a cuppa in one hand and a hot meat-pie in the other. 'How d'ya get on?'

I shrugged my shoulders.

'Got a real crush on her?' he asked.

'How d'you do?'

He grinned. 'OK, she's not my type really, she's good-looking though. Now, that Ruby Lestoque ... ' He named a school phenomenon in the second year.

'But she can only be eleven or twelve.'

'I know, but have you seen the form on her?' He chewed his pie lasciviously. 'I've got plans for her – I think everybody has, that's the trouble.'

'You can't let me down with Maureen, Ted.'

'Just take her out on yer own.'

'Well, I don't know if she'd go, let's fix up another foursome.'

'OK, just one.'

'Let's take 'em up West, you know a proper date.'

'You got any money?'

'I can raise a couple of quid.'

'You're on, I'll fix it up with Maureen.'

He did too. It turned out that the other Terry was away from school; his parents had taken him away on holiday. (With his *own* passport, it was rumoured abroad.)

Our date was set for the following Saturday. We met the girls at the Greengate bus stop, just in front of the Castle, a pub that was on the junction of Prince Regent's Lane and Barking Road. Opposite the Lane side of the pub was Larkin's the sweet shop which had recently opened an extension to sell just ice-cream. It was the first ice-cream shop in the neighbourhood and still a novelty. It was always a long wait to catch a 15 or a 23, so we bought the girls cornets, and Teddy and I had wafers. That was a shilling gone from the £2 I had borrowed from my classmate, Bill Cook. However, the finances of the excursion were not the foremost worry of the day. I had spent hours in front of the mirror above the sink in our scullery doing my hair with a new green brilliantine which came in an oval tin and smelt of lavender. That and my second Dayton roll, white, which my mum had rinsed in Reckitt's Blue and had a murderous time ironing. I couldn't get the knot of my tie right either. Dad passed through going to and fro from his shed, and the second time, I overheard him say to Mum, 'What's up with Lord Flaunt today?'

He meant Freddie Bartholomew in *Little Lord Fauntleroy*. It seems dumb now that at the time I imagined they didn't have a clue about what was going on. Teddy, of course, turned up just wearing his school threads so I felt uncomfortably overdressed although both girls looked smart. Toni had on higher heels than usual; they made her tanned legs taut. When we were strolling around St James's Park deciding what to do, I was aware of grown-up guys giving her the once-over.

Rainbow Corner was really packed out so we moseyed around the Circus and settled on the restaurant next to the Criterion Theatre – the Cri, as it was called – which seemed reasonable but was beautiful inside, with high mirrored alcoves and tiled floor. We all had fish from the self-service with real coffee which I thought sophisticated. It came to 7/6d each. Toni seemed interested seeing me eat my slice of lemon so, at her instigation, I stoically ate the other three pieces. They all pulled faces watching me, the atmosphere softened and we spent a long time drinking our coffees, leaning back in our chairs and gazing up at the twinkling gold and turquoise mosaic ceiling. Right at the start of Shaftesbury Avenue was a cartoon cinema where you paid and immediately went downstairs. Big and subterranean inside, it showed a whole programme of cartoons and that's where we went on that Saturday evening. It was 1/6d each, so even if Teddy didn't pay the bus ride home, I wasn't going to run out of cash.

When we got into the cinema proper there were no empty seats. We were shown to the back where we all leaned against the wooden division behind the back row. Toni was to my right with Maureen next to her and Teddy on the outside. The beam from the projector flickered over our heads and, although it was dark in the cinema, I could just see Toni's profile. The moment had come. I knew I should do something but I couldn't. Suddenly Maureen reached across her friend, took hold of my wrist and placed my arm around Toni's waist. One part of my hand could feel the shiny patent of her belt, the other the material of her blouse and the smoothness of her skin through it. The cartoon finished, the lights went up and strains of Leroy Anderson's 'Blue Tango' came over the speakers. I didn't want to move. People were leaving and we were shown to some vacant seats. But that moment, that song! Not 'Rhapsody in Blue', 'Serenade in Blue' or even 'Blue Champagne'; nope, it is plain ole 'Blue Tango' that still sends a recoil through my body. We came home via Aldgate, stopping off in Petticoat Lane for a tea at the coffee stall which Teddy knew: he was a great one for nocturnal tea spots. By the time we boarded the number 40 bus at its Aldgate turnaround, it was dark. We were the only passengers. We sat in state upstairs and, as we travelled right through the district where I first lived, I was able to make the others laugh by pointing out and mispronouncing the names of the old Jewish shops, Knopp and Lipschitz and so on. I hadn't seen Toni as animated as she was on this long bus ride, and I kept wondering if I could summon the courage to kiss her goodnight.

Years later I was to come across others of this feminine archetype, including geishas and modern courtesans, but that night I was just stumbling headlong into the space Toni's passivity created. Not yet having mastered being slow while feeling hot, I didn't read the language of this Jemal maiden, as they say in the desert of someone who embodies the aspect of a new moon.

The air in Beaumont Road was warm and again heavy with chrysanthemums. I linked hands with her and she didn't withdraw. I opened the gate of 36 and walked with her to the porch. The light was shining through the patterned glass window of the front door. I stood close to her, took her by her arms and leaned forward to kiss her, but she leaned back and for a second it crossed my mind that she was avoiding my embrace. I kept leaning; I couldn't have stopped. As I reached over her so our mouths could touch, she settled her bowed body into mine. I felt her stretched softness close into me. I made to grip her back in order to press her harder to me, but she disengaged herself and said, 'I must go in now.' There was an underlying finality in the way she said those words.

It was more final than I thought. The next week Terry Curtis was back at school and back with Toni. It didn't take him long to get wind of our flirtation and sort me out; he actually stopped me in the corridor and warned me off. It was the first of my unrequited love affairs.

For the next few weeks I hung around near Toni's home, hoping to catch her unaccompanied. The chrysanthemums were still there but I could no longer smell them on the air. I was in for a lot of this heartache before my teens were through, but as Granny Kate used to say, 'Whenever a door closes a window opens.'

Ten

DREAM IN ONE HAND

Above: A dab hand on the putting green

Our end of the road had two enviable features. The first thing was the water hydrant, which was the centre of the game 'Tin Can Tommy' and resembled a lamp-post whose growth had been stunted. Street-cleaning lorries would regularly dock alongside it to refill, attaching a metal-ended canvas hose to its circular mouth. There was more to this operation than met the eye, as so many passers-by got unexpectedly soaked during it. As soon as the lorry approached we would all congregate on Georgie Smith's coping just waiting to see people being caught unawares. The second feature was the wall of the Hobbses' house. This house occupied the corner of Chadwin and Egham Roads but, as the ground on which it stood didn't allow it to match either terrace, the developers had compromised and come up with a design which put its front window on Egham and a front door at the side of the house on Chadwin, although its postal address was 13 Egham Road. The side wall rose directly up from the pavement. When we lived in Bow, a detailed pecking order was designated according to the area or space in front of the houses. At the top of the list was the one generous enough to incorporate a privet hedge or flower-bed. Next was the concrete area a foot or so wide between the low brick wall and the window-sill. The houses everyone looked down on had front doors which opened directly on to the street. This concept was left behind when we moved to Plaistow. Areas were then assessed by us on functionality alone. Although our area was unusually wide, it wasn't favoured at all. The extra width prevented feet from being rested on the cement coping of our front wall while seated on the window-sill, added to which it was in shadow most of the day. Although Georgie Smith's and Tony Hughes's houses on the other side of the road had barely twelve inches of area, they had wonderful window-sills to lounge on and the low coping provided a surprisingly good hiding place when we lay down behind it in our versions of Ringolevio. But the Hobbses' wall was our most prized item; despite its chequered provenance, the twenty feet of uninter-rupted two-storeyed windowless bricks was a prime attraction. Endless cricket stumps were drawn on it during summer months and Martin Peters, who lived opposite in Number 85 with his gran, practised his illustrious sharp shooting, banging goals home be-tween the chalky posts long before Wembley in '66. The third sport which we practised endlessly, using the wall as a backdrop, and which started us early as sado-masochists, entailed a chosen 'shooter' who hurled a tennis ball at the rest of us 'targets' lined up against the wall. Whoever was hit by the ball was 'out'. Nobody ever heard Mr or Mrs Hobbs complain, but the interior side of the wall, their sitting-room, must definitely have been a 'no-go' area. The Hobbs family were tradespeople; they were affable enough but kept themselves to themselves. A lorry sometimes went through the big double doors into the yard that was next to our house. Mrs Hobbs also allowed me to climb over her back fence to get indoors when Ethel and Mrs Straffon were out. It was the Hobbses' telephone that was unstintingly used to relay messages to the family later on when great news started coming.

I don't know how an offer of a job came about, but it was probably elicited by Mum recounting my teenage gloom to Mrs Hobbs. One of their businesses was greengrocery and it was run by their son or son-in-law. I was to be a weekend apprentice and give a hand. The two guys who picked me up in the lorry at five a.m, that first Saturday morning certainly didn't need the help of my soft hand but seemed to relish the prospect of a mascot. It was still dark when they bundled me into the cabin of the Dodge. I sat between the two of them, on a cushion warm from the engine, and they gave me a swig of hot, sweet tea from a wire-top bottle. It was strong and made with evaporated milk. What a luxury! We only ever had it with jelly on a Sunday. We went somewhere in the dark to load up with fruit and veg, then stopped at street markets and shops to drop off produce. I stayed in the back perched on the boxes for this part of the trip, letting down the tailboard whenever we made a delivery and hauling whatever it was they wanted into the back so they didn't have to keep climbing up themselves. What an amazing day that was, amidst the pineapples, tangerines and bananas; all stuff I usually only got to look at. I had my first pomegranate that day. Thrust into my hand by a big raw-boned woman we delivered to. She must have seen me gaze longingly at a basketful with one on top pulled apart and showing its exotic seeds, like something from Ali Baba's cave. Driving home, work done, back in the cabin, I kept taking it out of my pocket, touching the rough skin and examining its ear still full of sawdust.

'Who gave you that then?' asked Jack, who was driving.

'The woman at the last drop.'

'You want to go easy with her, she'll eat you without salt.' They both chuckled.

'What d'you mean?' It sounded somehow not too bad.

'She's a real performer. I remember before she got hitched . . . '
He went on to recount a tale of flicking his scarf like a towel on her
backside as she bent over a pile of potatoes. 'King Edwards, as it
happened. This went on for a few weeks, one thing led to another,
scarf to hand, handful, hand full and a Midland.'

'Midland?' I queried.

'Yeah, Midland Bank.' He gestured the meaning of the rhyming
slang, taking his hand off the wheel. 'Finally, in the back on sacks
and cauliflowers.'

I tried to look blasé. 'Performer, eh?'

'Blinder,' said Jack, winking at me and his mate. 'Keep it to
yourself though, I mean she's a happily married woman now.'

'Yeah,' said his mate, 'save the occasional fresh one with rosy
cheeks, eh?'

I did blush a bit then; not that I believed a word about her
fancying me, but it did make me feel good to be treated like one of
them, one of the lads. I couldn't believe it when Jack pressed four
half crowns into my hand when they dropped me off at the lido,
waving through the window with a cheery, 'Same time next
Saturday then, sailor!' I'd have paid them, come to think of it. It
amazed me how good I felt getting up at five a.m., so different from
my last attempt at working life. No more Saturday morning
pictures followed by saveloys and pease pudding for me. I did that
job right up until Christmas, having a whale of a time and earning
enough to score myself a complete new outfit in time for the school
dance.

Preparations for this annual ritual were under way halfway
through term. One of our two weekly PT periods was spent in the
assembly hall trying to teach us how to dance under the all-seeing
evil eye of Mr Priest who was almost as uncomfortable as we were.
Also trying to push us together in pairs was a girls' teacher, whose
only memorable feature was legs which bore a distinct resemblance
to Reg Harris's, the then world champion cyclist. These monu-
ments were housed in a short pleated navy skirt which showed off
their vastness. As dance instruction was given in a PT period, and
as it would have killed Priest to let us learn to dance in street
clothes, we had to change into our gym kit as usual. A motley array
of skinny white limbs in wide dark shorts and singlets stood around
the extremities of the hall, mostly down the side furthest away from

where the girls congregated. There was no competition between the two sexes in the looks department. Obviously a fifteen-year-old girl is nearing perfect bloom, while boys are a spotty valley of transformation. Apart from this, our togs were just the pits. None of us had anything that wasn't improvised and certainly there was no sign of the regulation white socks; the poorer kids didn't have shorts and made do with underwear with the crotches sewn up. The holey greasy plimsolls that had never known blanco, matched the rolled-down grey school socks which acted as a gesture of revolt in a boys only class.

We were so scared of Priest and forgetting our togs on gym days that most of us kept our stuff compressed into our desks for terms at a time, so you can imagine our odour wasn't exactly peachy. Not even Priest's glare could induce any of us voluntarily to choose a partner for the Veleta. Teachers formed us into two circles with the girls on the inside and then we were made to step out in opposite directions so that we partnered whoever was nearest when the music stopped. We were drilled through the Veletas, Gay Gordons and Boston Two-Steps, progressive and otherwise. These turgid periods were lightened by seeing Priest in his immaculate drill trousers like some ascetic monk, and his discomfort at having actually to hold a woman infinitely more serious than our worries about bony knees.

That Christmas Dance was memorable. I wore a pearl-grey suit with a maroon shirt and silver tie, but despite my flash get-up I was a bit self-conscious when it came to actually launching myself. Warren Hopps arrived to find me skulking outside so he wheeled me in with him. He said, 'Wow, that is some outfit,' and I felt like Jack the lad. I had mentioned the dance to Roy during the week and he said he might look in. To my surprise and delight, he did. The glory, albeit reflected, that I soaked in that night! The girls of my own year had hardly ever given me the time of day, preferring to chatter loudly about sixth-form prefects, all of eighteen, who were 'cool' and brainy enough to stay on an extra two years and take 'A' levels. Now these same mature customers were all over me like a rash in quivering groups, fillies having their first glimpse at a stallion. Roy, Ken and the other Terry refused to take part in any old-time dances and girls were actually asking me to dance to find out who this guy was. It was only when Ted Heath's new tune came on to the record player that Roy invited Barbara Say on to the floor, and introduced her and us to 'the Creep'. He was just the most laid-back guy I'd ever met, actually stopping dancing during the number and engaging her in chat in the middle of the floor. I can honestly say that Roy's problems with girls appeared to be absolutely non-existent. He really played the field that night and, although none in particular caught the Irish Sea eyes, we all strolled up to Plaistow Station with a group from my class who lived out Forest Gate way – Barbara, Kay Vincent and Jean Appleton, who the other Terry thought had a terrific backside. At the 699 stop on top of the hill outside the station, Roy tightened his tie, turned up the hand-stitched collar of his jacket and shook hands, rather formally I thought, with the girls when the trolley bus arrived. They all said how much they'd enjoyed the evening, be nice to meet again, but Roy didn't speak; he just grinned in a friendly way, showing the gums of his top teeth.

Ken and Terry got on the bus and Roy and I strolled back down the hill and cut through Balaam Street past the public baths. Roy seemed rather talkative, he thought the dance a real laugh, and then he said, 'I didn't see you on the floor much. Don't you have anybody there you fancy?'

'There is a girl I like but she wasn't there tonight. She has a fella anyway.'

'Yeah, well plenty more fish in the sea.'

He crooned a few bars of 'That's Amore', accentuating the roll of his shirt collar the way Dean Martin did. He said, 'I'd really like to get some of those shirts he wears.'

'Probably gets them made special,' I said. 'In Hollywood.'

''Spect so.'

'What are you going to do, Roy, when you leave school?' I didn't expect him to tell, but as he seemed so accessible I thought I'd ask.

'I haven't really thought about it yet; just figured I'd get these GCEs over!'

As I'd anticipated, he was playing it close to the chest – he who travels alone travels quickest. We had reached the Staddon's corner. Opposite the Abbey Arms, where Mum had barmaided between kids, the last drinkers were leaving. Roy stopped and faced me, but I could see that his mind was on other things. He said, 'I have to knuckle down to revision for these exams; I won't be up the club so much for a bit.'

I nodded.

'What's she called, the girl that you like?'

'She's called Ethel but only answers to Toni.'

'Yeah.' He smiled, considering this new fact, and was about to continue when I burst out, 'I'm so jealous. I run into them all the time.'

Roy didn't speak. I wished I hadn't spoken; the silence became awkward, and if I'd been able to smoke this was a moment I'd have filled by lighting up a fag. Instead I said, 'Don't you ever get jealous, Roy?'

'Over girls?'

'Yeah – girls.'

He sort of rubbed the dimple in his chin – it was already blue – and then in a rather measured way he said, 'Only enough to reassure 'em.'

I've become rather a fan of Tom Selleck lately. I often catch *Magnum Private Investigator*. His personality reminds me of Roy Studd's. They don't look alike; there is just a similar kind of sweetness, or *dolcissimo* as they say in Italy.

In the summer of '53 my brother Chris passed his eleven-plus, so as I moved up into the fifth form, Chris started his first year at Plaistow, and Richard, now seven, inherited Mr Newby at Tolgate. The same Eric Newby who had coached me and brought us conkers in the autumn. He always said he just picked them up on his way to work. As he lived in Wanstead, I formed all kinds of mental pictures of this district, along much the same lines as Dick Whittington's imaginings about London. So when brother Richard came home from school one lunch-time and relayed the possibility of a part-time job for me at Newby's local golf club, I was all ears. I had never had any reason to venture into the svelte residential district beyond the Flats. The Wanstead Flats, a big expanse of common land encompassing woods, ponds and grazing land, were reserved for Bank Holidays, gypsy fun-fairs, newting trips or special outings to watch trainee parachutists. I knew that it was Winston Churchill's constituency; the very heart of bluest Conservatism where everyone had cars, TV sets and even billiard tables, and where full-grown chestnut trees lined the avenues.

'You sure he said me?' I wanted to know.

'Hmm,' he answered. Richard was already showing signs of being a considerable Stoic.

'Me, he asked me?'

'Yeah, told ya.'

'What exactly did he say, Rich?'

Richard rubbed the top of his summer crew-cut that Chris and I had masterminded. It hadn't grown out. I waited, feeling my life could be about to change.

'He said, "If your eldest brother would like to help out at Wanstead Golf Club evenings and weekends, 'e should go and see the pro there. They're looking for someone."'

The effort seemed to have drained him; he went into the scullery to see how Ethel was doing at the gas cooker. I looked to Chris for an opinion; he was lounging in the best armchair on the right of the fireplace. This chair was the most sought after for two reasons; it was in the corner that had the light and view from the only window in the room, and was the one comfortable spot where the ailing wireless could generally be heard. The valves of this contraption were something Dad intended to replace when his ship came in – won the pools – even before going on a luxury cruise to think about how to spend the bulk of the money. Chris didn't seem interested enough to offer an opinion. I moved into the radius of the feeble airwaves, intending to trick Chris into giving up his seat.

Mum shouted from the scullery, 'Wait till the food's on the table!' and Richard appeared at the door, his mouth full of hot chips, saying, ' . . . said they'd teach you golf . . . 'stead of wages!'

Chris narrowed his eyes. They were lighter than mine and already showing a certain steeliness, a quality recognised by the Rock and Roll Raj of the Sixties, who named him 'the grey wolf'. He said, 'Don't sound much cop to me, playing golf for nothink; you can play football in the street for nothink.'

There wasn't much I could say to Chris at the time; four years my junior, but already so smart and more mature than myself in many ways. I couldn't have explained the dream I held in one hand, the mistake I felt my surroundings to be, or the ever-increasing tightness around me, a barrier impervious to my efforts to break through or climb over. This offer, coming as it did out of the blue, might be the chink in the wall. I had always thought of Fate, when it finally came for me, taking me west to the lights and incident of the West End, but I couldn't pass up a chance even if it was only a number 40 bus going farther east into E11. Most of my youth was spent vacillating between insecurity and confidence. I can't say it ever occurred to me that there was anything unusual in my condition, or that it was in my hands to do anything about it. Some situations made me feel up; some took away all my gumption. I didn't question either state. The job at the golf club which I scuttled off to after school would have answered all my prayers if I had been able to master the game, but this proved to be the central flaw. Everything else was just terrific. Reg Knight, the pro, was gentle and caring. He had two full-time assistants, Keith Hockey and Peter Shanks, the latter of whom was only three years older than me. All three were athletes with differing good-looks, and the sum of masculine appeal when they were all together in the little shop often made a visible impact on the tweedy ladies who came in to pick up their clubs or buy equipment, and frequently dallied while doing so.

I had approached the club along Overton Drive the first time, peering through the fence at the lake which made up the course's only water hole and taking the first sign to turn right into what turned out to be the club's back entrance. Summer had come late that year and everything was still and green. The footpath was a leafy corridor with sounds of flying insects and tennis games in progress off to the right. The air felt soft. The trees opened on to what I assumed was the start of a golf course, and I saw two ladies standing on a raised grass rectangle with golf bags on carry-carts. One had just hit a ball and the other was bending over and placing a golf ball on a little wooden peg. I stopped as she addressed the ball and hit it towards the green in the distance. It didn't look too difficult. She turned to face me and said, 'How was that?' It took me a moment to realise that she was speaking to me. I must have been staring at her. I just nodded my head in a gormless sort of way. She smiled and the two of them walked off. She had a fine prominent nose and a voice which sounded like an announcer on the wireless. I followed a little sign to the clubhouse, up a narrow path. It is hard to forget my first vision of that building. Whole parts of it were covered in ivy, some turning red, and big open sash windows overlooked a manicured nine-hole putting green. I soon realised that I was looking at the back of the club but this enclave came to represent something I hadn't felt before. It got so I could hardly wait to finish school lessons to get there.

A rather muscular young guy with his sleeves rolled up was hitting half a dozen balls one after the other towards a hole with a metal flag. He had that kind of dark ash-blond hair that women often covet. He holed his last ball and I said, 'Where is the pro shop?'

He grinned; it made him look wicked like Kirk Douglas. 'You're standing in front of it, who d'you want?'

So impressed had I been by the aesthetics of the clubhouse, I had walked right past the series of huts which formed a wooden arm to the main building.

'The pro, I've come to see the pro.'

He picked up a small yellow bag with a circular mouth and, using his club face, flicked the balls into it without bending.

'You've come about the job? My name is Peter Shanks, I'm the second assistant.' He offered me a strong weatherbeaten hand and gripped mine just hard enough to let me know that he could have crushed it if he'd wanted to. It was the start of a friendship, firm like his grip.

Reg Knight OKed me. He looked a dreamy sort of guy, but he was a scratch golf pro, with a perfect swing that had been taught to him by Henry Cotton. His first assistant, Keith, destined to follow the sun since birth – he'd been christened Keith Ryder – was one of those heroic creatures I imagined Biggles to be, caring and supportive, giving me a wooden-shafted five iron and my initial lesson on the fairway nearest the clubhouse. But Peter became the first in a succession of initiators into the mysteries of adult life.

I had never thought of myself as an athlete. I didn't have any outstanding natural ability and any compulsions weren't aroused until later in life. Miranda Coe, Seb's breathtaking sister, told me she couldn't remember her brother ever walking when they were out as children; he would run on ahead and then run back. I was good at high-jump but I didn't practise; I just threw myself over the bar on sports days. Peter Shanks was the first professional athlete I knew, and contact with him brought home a number of revelations. The first was that you could make a living doing something you enjoyed, and that it could be *physical*. Dad's daily labours looked like drudgery to me. My schooling had confirmed it. Using muscle meant labouring – bad; passing exams and becoming qualified by using brains – good. Mr Priest did make a living by physical activities, but then nobody in their right mind would have been inspired by him. I don't know how Peter became so good so young. His social graces could not have made any impression in genteel golf circles. At heart he was a bit of a wide-boy, but members

Above: Born to swing: Peter Shanks

respected him, and the stockbrokers and estate agents who were his peers acknowledged that he could always take their money even while giving them strokes. He was tough on me, ridiculing my romantic attitudes and making me face up to my lack of drive and confidence. He reckoned you could get whatever you wanted if you paid the price of the ticket, which often meant coldly assessing your ability and galvanising yourself to act.

Using the green in front of the shop at slack times when chores like cleaning the members' shoes and clubs were out of the way, I became adept at putting. Acquiring a rhythmic swing and hitting the ball accurately – if at all – was another matter. Reg and the boys were not heavy on me for being such a clutz, and at weekends time was made for me to take my five iron and a bag containing fifty practice balls to knock back and forth on the practice ground. That was until we discovered a full-size Jacques table-tennis table stored away in one of the winter practice sheds, and I gave Peter and a few other guys a real thrashing. Then Peter got on my case.

'If you're that good at ping-pong, you can be that good at golf,' he rasped at me. 'Don't give me that wilting violet act. Your eyes are sharp as a razor; you just don't want to work, that's the strength of it.'

I mumbled about not knowing how and he said, 'The difference between amateurs and guys who do it for a living is that they play in their spare time and we practise. Practice ain't so much fun but,' he paused, 'you've got to put your money where your mouth is.'

In the members' wash-room one time after work he was introducing me to the mysteries of Amami setting lotion. Putting a green dollop on his hair, he said, 'What are you doing about National Service?'

I said that I couldn't even think about it.

'That's no good, if you don't think about it they'll have you in before your feet can touch the ground: two years wasted, learning how to march, polish buttons and shoot people.'

'What are you doing?'

'Don't worry about me, sunshine. You give it some thought – two years out of your life's a big slice.'

It was only when I left school and life started rushing towards me that I began to ponder 'putting my money where my mouth was' and how best to use my time. People I admired did appear to have in common the ability to apportion time. Peter always appeared to enjoy what he was doing without being under pressure to be somewhere else. One evening, at a summer table between the club and the putting green, tucking into the soft roes on toast that Peter had treated us to, I asked him about the knack of not being rushed.

'I don't allow myself to be rushed. Rushing – that's for slaves, not princes!'

Yeah, I'd stumbled on another prince all right. There he was, brown as a nut, forearms and wrists like iron, relaxed and in charge of himself and all he surveyed. That year he took me to watch the Ryder Cup at Wentworth's Burma Road. He was a great fan of American golfers and appreciated everything from their playing action to their colourful gear. We were watching Cary Middlecoff hit a long second shot and I queried his choice of iron which I thought was low for such a windy moment. Shanks just said, 'It's windy here, but look at the flag.'

Sure enough, the flag on the pin was dead.

Above: Not born to swing: Terence Stamp

Dream in One Hand

The job at Wanstead took most of my interest. This new world was so intoxicating that I couldn't summon any energy to put into my work at school, even with my GCE year approaching. Although in my heart of hearts I knew I could never be good enough to make my living by playing golf, I was overwhelmed by a reckless desire to burn my bridges before getting even a glimmer of what lay ahead.

I had failed to be chosen by Miss Wilks for her school production of *Tom Sawyer*. In fact my mate, Teddy Debell, had landed the plum role so I went to see the show. Something I saw that night made me sour with envy. There was a scene with Tom and Huck in the carriage of a train. At the start of the piece they had to mime in unison to convey the motion. The stage lighting narrowed in on them as the train started. They did it so well, using their swaying to accentuate the delivery of their words so expertly that they gripped the whole audience. Everyone became of a oneness, sharing in that pretended moment. Everyone, that is, except me. My discontent set me apart. I wasn't content to be a part of it, and to be passive.

Eleven

SHANGRI-LA

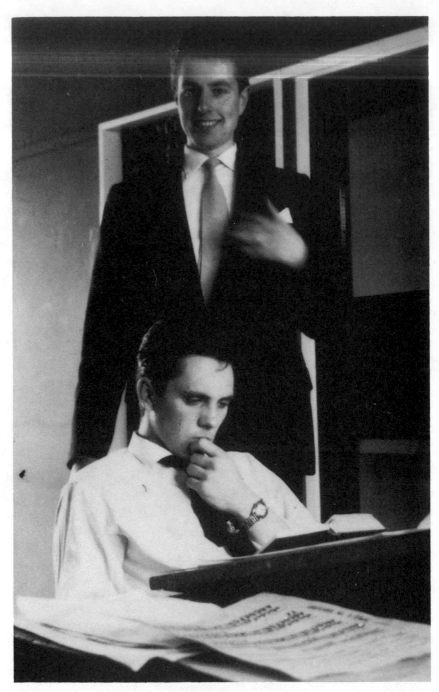

Above: At Napper, Stinton and Wooley with Barry

My die was cast for good shortly afterwards. I went to Fairbairn one night when I wasn't needed at the golf club and ran into Roy. He was playing darts on the first floor. He looked terrific as usual, and was basking in the satisfaction of having passed lots of GCEs. I carried my five iron everywhere like a walking-stick to practise the hand-strengthening exercise that Shanks had given me, and Roy was impressed at the fact that I was learning how to play golf, especially as it was Dean Martin's hobby. I used the moment to ask Roy what he was going to do now that he had completed school. He said he was taking the summer holidays off, but I wasn't deterred. I'd been waiting a long time to see Roy's first move towards the lights. I said, 'Good idea, but you know, what about work?'

'Oh, all taken care of.' He grinned slowly. 'My dad's got me started at the Paragon.'

'The Paragon?' I repeated the name of the big local printing company.

'Yeah, you know – I'm going to learn typesetting, seven-year apprenticeship.'

I looked at him as if he were pulling my leg, but he was obviously not. It was, after all, a very good number by Plaistow standards, but I was in shock for days. If Roy, Roy who had it all, who could do just about everything, was settling for a slow climb up the traditional ladder, what chance did someone like me have? I was suddenly in the dark with no one to point the way. It slowly dawned on me that Roy might not have the vain-glorious ambitions I had always attributed him with. It was a long time before I saw that he hadn't needed the kind of reassurance I was seeking. I didn't realise how much I looked to him for guidance, until I understood that I could no longer follow. I was on my own.

In a moment of derangement I heard that the East Ham Dramatic and Choral Society were looking for a player to complete their cast of *The Sacred Flame* by Somerset Maugham. They were in dire straits, a last-minute drop-out I imagine, because they happily accepted me for the part of a 65-year-old colonel. It was a big part, a very big part, and it involved practically finishing the third act single-handed, or so it seemed at the time. It was a way of justifying my almost certain failure to pass any GCEs. Now my time was completely taken up by the job at Wanstead and learning the lines of the play. I don't know how I ever learnt the part, let alone got on. I spent those spring months of '54 in a frenzy, torn in three directions, my three possible life paths, as it were. On 23 July, the day after my sixteenth birthday when my frenetic efforts fizzled out, I was still none the wiser. Predictably I had failed every one of my GCEs, even art which I'd always been good at. I hadn't been able to apply myself enough to give Reg Knight the confidence to employ me full-time at the golf club, and *The Sacred Flame* had been a nightmare. The public dress rehearsal in front of the Deaf, Dumb and Blind Association had been almost as unnerving as the performance the following night at East Ham Town Hall. In the last act I had succumbed so fully to nerves that I started stuttering and transposing words in my dialogue which effectively made absolute gibberish of the text, let alone the plot. The final blow came when I discovered that the drama critic of the *Stratford Express* had been present and said in his review: 'The cast was uniformly good with the exception of Terence Stamp; never did he appear convincing as a man with years of service in the Army. This character jarred; the lines he spoke clashing with his shock of black hair . . . ' I had dabbed a little talcum powder on my sideboards as a token of maturity. It was a look I'd seen Stewart Granger effect that I was rather taken with but which, along with a walking-stick I'd used for hobbling about the stage, hadn't impressed the *Stratford Express* which just about everybody took. All kinds of kids I'd never dreamt could read brought me cuttings 'just in case I'd missed it'. Overall, the experience was so awesome that I swore it would be the last theatrical escapade I would ever embark on. *The Sacred Flame* sure extinguished any sparks I had in that direction.

Mum pushed me off to the Youth Employment Bureau where a rather sympathetic man asked me which subjects had interested me at school. I told him art, drama and probably English. From that meagre information he gathered that a career in advertising would be right up my street. He produced a white card bearing the name Wilkes Bros & Greenwood, Cheapside, who were looking for a trainee copywriter. I took the 23 bus, got off at Mappin & Webb and walked up Cheapside to Friday House. An elegant lift of polished wood took me at a dignified pace to the fourth floor. A real piece called Marion directed me through a sliding wooden panel to a Mr Baker's office. I could see her crossing and uncrossing her legs, perched on a revolving stool in a tight skirt. Before she closed the oak partition, she managed to slick another coat of Sudden Death Red on to her lips. A prick-tease, I thought, mentally consulting Shanks's dictionary of sexual archetypes. Strictly look, no touch, ole Marion.

Mr Baker was a stout, ebullient type, with flattened curly hair, a moustache and bright elastic braces. He interviewed me, or rather he told me what I'd be doing. It sounded like messenger boy cum filing clerk to me. I said, 'What about the copywriting?'

'It pays three pounds a week,' he continued, 'with luncheon vouchers.'

Luncheon vouchers! I'd thought often enough if it gets worse when I leave school I'll kill myself. That day I thought I might have to do it.

'Oh, how many GCEs did you get?' Mr Baker said as I was leaving his office to give my particulars to a Miss Robbins, his secretary next door.

I worked out how many I needed to deliver parcels. 'Eight,' I said, getting into the swing of advertising.

Of course, Ethel was delighted. I'd got the first job I'd tried for. None the less, I felt on edge that evening. Chris was plastering a doorstep of bread with dripping. Richard was testing his night vision in the cupboard under the stairs where you needed clair-voyance even to find your coat. Dad was at the front door explaining to a Jehovah's Witness that he couldn't subscribe today as he'd only just come out of prison, and Mum was whistling up my favourite egg and chips. All in all, another day at 124. But something was taking place in my head. A kind of recognition that a big slice of my life was over, and although I hadn't liked it much it was already exerting a pull on me. Even at scrawny sixteen, the past was becoming a mistress that both repelled and attracted me.

For the rest of that week I wandered around my old haunts, the Rec., the dumps. I even squeezed myself into a pull-up baby swing in a deserted rainy Beckton Park, knowing my boyhood was gone and not wanting to admit it. I visited the attic of the bandstand where Teddy and I had stored the bulbs, plundered from the gardens to resell in the spring but never collected. I returned to Rosseta Road School sports ground where they'd tried to teach me the Western Roll so I could jump for my County. It was all there, all much the same. I stared as though to devour it, to inhale it all in so deep as to make it part of me. Come next week it would never be the same.

In the end, the transition to work was almost painless. It was almost without excitement too, and that was the problem. I think Mum must have wanted to give me some of her Leonine vigour that first morning. She was up long before me and, by the time I'd finished my wash in the scullery, she had tea and toast on the table with the first of the damson jam we'd made the night before. It was seven-thirty; we ate our breakfast together. This became a ritual between us whenever I had to face big steps in my life.

There is a puzzling connection I have with our house in Chadwin Road. Beautiful it wasn't; I don't remember it having any pleasing qualities at all, with its small rooms and steep, dangerous stairs. But in those dream states when I'm about to have a dream that is more than just the brain chattering to itself, it always begins at 124, with me either standing outside in the porch looking down at the front step with its red, black and biscuit harlequin tiles and entering the dingy passage, or finding myself in our lop-sided lino-covered living-room.

On this, my first morning before work, when Mum joined me at table, I sat against the wall under the plaster Alsatian dog I'd won at Beckton Fair and she sat opposite me. I could see part of her reflection in the new Ferguson TV set we'd just acquired on HP. I wasn't nervous; it was just like going to school, only earlier – the first black mark against it. On other occasions when Mum was psyching me up, she was chatty, often using strong gestures. This time, however, she seemed subdued, just watching me. Her thoughts came into my head as though she was thinking aloud. I silently tried to reassure her. She had brought me up right. I could go it alone.

When I was ready to leave the house, she handed me a pack of sandwiches, cheese and sweet pickle. I expected her to say, 'Don't do anything I wouldn't do,' or some such adage. Instead, at the street door she said, 'Your grandad used to say that anything you set out to do that you don't finish is bigger than you, but you are bigger than anything you finish properly.'

The most practical route to Wilkes Bros would have been a number 699 to Plaistow Underground and then District Line to Mansion House, but that morning I needed all the comfort I could get. I left the trolley at Greengate and caught a 15. The bus wasn't full and I took the corner seat on the bench and paid the full fare of 6d. I kept getting this picture of my gran, as though she was sitting with me. When I got off at Bank, I realised that I had rolled my ticket into a tight little ball.

Marion, the telephone operator and receptionist, turned out to be friendly, though my first instinct about her was right; she had a regular boyfriend, on promise, doing his stint in the Army.

Mr Baker never came in until eleven. He shared his office with Mr Sherlock, a diminutive art director. Mr Baker called him Shylock. They laughed a lot and reminded me of Laurel and Hardy.

Wilkes Bros and Greenwood occupied a suite of offices in Friday House which stood on the west side of Cheapside, between Friday Street and Bread Street where the Great Fire is alleged to have started. I don't know when it was built, but it was outfitted in the Twenties when a degree of importance was still attached to physical surroundings. The floors were parquet and the space was partitioned by wooden-panelled walls. I was given a place in the general office which housed the reception area and three desks. A boy called Clifford had one desk, and the largest, with a big drawing board, was waiting for a Roy who was doing his National Service. This main room adjoined the studio, shared by two guys, Basil and Glyn, who did the artwork. On the other side of the short corridor was Accounts, the boss's room, and the anteroom, which he shared with Shylock. I was given a tobacco tin with a £5 float in it for travel, which I duly itemised. Clifford showed me the filing system.

The first few weeks were uneventful. I spent most of my time delivering metal blocks to the Fleet Street offices of provincial newspapers. The major clients of Mr Baker were Vedonis, a manufacturer of ladies' underwear with cotton inside and wool outside ('Next to myself I like Vedonis'), and Knitmaster, the first of the knitting machines ('Knit faster with Knitmaster'). Knitmaster had a showroom in Bond Street with lots of pretty demonstrators. I didn't mind delivering there. The account I really liked was A.C. Cars. They had a factory at Tags Island, which involved a train ride to Thames Ditton, and quite the most glamorous cars I'd ever seen. At first the deliveries were fun. I was provided with an *A – Z* and an Underground map, and as far as I was concerned this was a luxurious way to learn the geography of the West End. I kept a notebook of locations that took my fancy, cobblers that made shoes and a little shop that had a suede waistcoat in the window. Oh yes, the biggest client was Singer sewing machines. Their building was at the top of Moorgate and during one of my errands I came upon an old tobacconist's that sold exotic cigarettes. I started effecting Turkish ovals and finally mastered 'taking it down'.

One afternoon I had to deliver an envelope to Davies Street. I looked it up in my *A – Z* and saw that the nearest tube was Green Park. I hadn't been to that station before and I remember thinking how nice it sounded. As I have mentioned, I'd always felt destined to wind up in Central London, so in my head I wasn't just delivering – I was getting to know my patch. Nobody at the agency seemed aware of my comings and goings, so if I lost my way I just wandered around, taking in the scene and making notes, until I found a bus route I knew or an Underground which would take me back to base. On that particular afternoon I emerged up the stairs from Green Park Station on to what I now know to be the north side of Piccadilly. It was a sunny day, tight and bright. I stopped to take in the panorama. I don't know what triggered it, the breeze riffling through the leaves of the big trees, the light on the buildings giving a luminosity to stone walls, but I was suddenly enveloped by a feeling of familiarity so strong that it pushed aside the logic confirming that I had never set foot on this spot before. The sensation accompanying this 'memory' seemed to take over my body as though an ancient door had opened, turning my blood to foam, and I gave in to the thrill and slumped against the wall next to the Underground exit.

Studying the scene in front of me, I began to divide it up – the tilting red telephone boxes, the fruit stall, the entrance to the park, the name Ritz on the white building – but, with the start of this mental search for the source of my state, the empathy with my surroundings faded. The glow left me and I continued leaning, feeling rather tender and becoming aware of the sounds of the street. I delivered my package and strolled around for a bit, taking in the elegance of the area, and then lost my way. I was heading towards the traffic noise of what I supposed was a main road, when I came upon an extremely quaint tobacco shop, its tiny shop-front set back to incorporate a bend in the pavement; its fraternal twin, a flower shop, was a few yards farther along separated by a set of black shutters. As I stepped back a pace to take in the shops together, a door that cut into the horizontal slats of the shutters suddenly swung open as if by itself and it was a good moment before a liveried porter in tall, crested topper came into frame carrying a suitcase.

In that moment a vision unrolled before me. It was as if I was looking into a tunnel that had become unexpectedly filled with light. On closer scrutiny, it was a covered walk about eight or nine foot wide. Beyond and parallel to the fine iron railings on each side of the walkway were trimmed privet hedges which accentuated the rolling decline of the arcade. Immediately beyond the privets was the building itself, painted white with high Georgian windows, each with individual boxes. The sunlight bounced off these walls, highlighting the oblong gardens between the hedges and the railings. These gardens housed clouds of pearly pink rhododendrons in wooden tubs. Supported by regular square posts at the corners, the roof of the walk branched out to cover the few feet to the entrance passages of the building, protecting but not separating the users from the elements. The whole thing appeared oriental. It brought to mind Besant's palace, where Tigerlily lived in my old Rupert annuals.

The burly porter was putting the suitcase into the boot of a red Austin Atlantic just down the street. I was tempted to step over the shutter frame through that opening, convinced for one mad moment that I would be transported into another dimension, just like Alice going through the looking-glass. I didn't. The porter returned. The door slammed shut.

I found a bus. It was too late to go back to the agency. I took a number 15 all the way to Greengate. I had been in such a daze that I hadn't made a note of a single street name. I didn't even know where this enclave was — let alone what. Over the years my impression of the stillness that seemed to be contained between those high walls was so strong that it came to represent a Shangri-la, a physical embodiment of a state within the world's buffeting, but not of it.

Twelve

SONGS OF
SWINGING
LOVERS

Above: Lechery at Butlin's

I settled into working life, getting a pay packet on Friday and giving Mum 30/- of it. I had joined another club: the YMCA. It was a big building in Greengate Street directly opposite the bus garage. It wasn't anywhere near as elegant as Fairbairn but I'd heard they had a crack table-tennis team, some boys even representing Essex. It was also a mixed club. As the job at Wilkes Bros didn't seem to be satisfying me any more than school, I took to spending almost all my spare time at the YMCA, practising endlessly on one of the six tables in the basement, and then jogging home to bed feeling absolutely wiped out. I made friends with a lot of guys who played there but one, Bernie Wilson, I took a special shine to. He was from up North, and his dad had been a fighter pilot in the Battle of Britain. Bernie's family lived on the Highway in Stepney, in a flat next to the Meredith & Drew factory where Bernie's dad was security officer. They were altogether a handsome family. Bernie had two elder sisters: Christina, who still lived at home, and Shelagh who was a fashion model, with her own agency in Manchester. Every year Shelagh's husband used to give Bernie his cast-off tailored shirts and one year Bernie gave one to me, a bright blue sea-island cotton with double cuffs and this chap's monogram on the sleeve. It wasn't what you'd call a bespoke fit, but I thought it just the polar bear's pyjamas.

Bernie had heard of a tailor in Brick Lane who cut suits as good as anything in Savile Row. He charged £20. Bernie's dad got us evening work frying crisps in M & D (3/- an hour) and we worked a couple of nights a week in order to save up. Charles Stevens's shop was in Brick Lane, just as Bernie had heard. It was opposite Marella Pickles and you could see their sign through the tailor's small shop-front. I remember it distinctly because I stood by the door in the dim store and looked out while Bernie negotiated with Mr Stevens. He had told me it was absolutely essential to bargain with Jews, or four by twos as we used to call them. According to him they expected it and walked all over you if you didn't. I was embarrassed and dreaded having to ask for a reduction when my turn came. I was saved from that when he and Bernie agreed on £18 'cash in hand'.

The master tailor turned to me and said, 'That goes for you too, I suppose?'

Bernie nodded furiously at me. I shrugged my shoulders and heard myself saying, 'I need handstitching.'

I ran my fingers down my obviously un-handstitched lapels.

Mr Stevens gestured scornfully at my jacket. 'I don't do anything on the engine.'

I guess I looked blank.

He hesitated. 'It's by hand, it's all done by hand, we don't do machine stuff. We don't do schmatah.'

He seemed rather bad-tempered, and I was having second thoughts about entrusting him with my first made-to-measure. I stopped trying to separate two pounds from the twenty in my trouser pocket without being noticed. But as soon as the deal had been done he became charm itself, standing on a stool, dropping on the wooden counter bolts of cloth which he pulled down from the shelves. Tweeds, hopsacks, gabardines of all shades and weights came thudding down on top of one another. Bernie grabbed a Prince of Wales check which he took to the door for a better look.

I was stopped in my tracks by the spectacle before me. Mr Stevens must have seen the bolt of serge that caught my eye. He said, 'Put yer hand in that,' jumping down and plunging his hand into the depths of the gun-metal grey to show me how.

I did as he said.

'Well, what d'you feel?'

'It's cool,' I replied.

'It's cold,' he said, 'and that's how you know a good worsted, a really good worsted. Cloth is like wine, a good cloth gets better as it gets older.'

'Does it?' I was on new ground here. My clothes just fell to pieces, even my corduroy trousers which I felt would last for ever.

'Feel the pukht.' He continued rubbing the cloth with a prac- tised thumb and forefinger. 'That's no mill finish, that's clean- cut. Pre-war. I reckon that would have made your dad a great whistle.' He fixed me with a beady eye. 'It'll make you a better one though. I'll make you a suit. You've got a long back, lets a jacket hang right.' He pulled a tape measure from his waistcoat pocket and measured the inside of my leg, mumbling something about dressing to the right, and then said, 'You've got a long leg as well!'

I was gently relieved of my coat as Mr Stevens seemed to memorise my shoulders with his smooth hands. Bernie, watching from the door, noted the look of bliss on my face and chuckled, 'Looks like you're getting a suit whether you like it or not.'

Charlie Stevens was as good as his word, although he didn't give me a velvet collar. 'Wot's a young gent like you want with looking like a teddy boy?'

He drew the line there, although he narrowed the trousers three inches to eighteen at my second Sunday morning fitting, and recommended a tobacco-brown silk lining instead of black: 'Then you can have a choice of shoes.'

It's not every guy whose first bespoke is a winner. In fact, some very fashionable tailors get away with charging a bomb for clothes that might have been cut for somebody else. But even the really good tailor, who prides himself on getting it right every time, occasionally comes up with an achievement that is something that stands apart. I asked my tailor in Rome (who made me the best linen suit ever, when I went to work for Fellini in '66) about this phenomenon. He had just completed a work of art out of an old piece of midnight-blue serge I'd come across when rummaging around his shop, just enough for a double-breasted two-piece. At the very first fitting I knew he'd got it right. You can always tell at the first fitting. I took the trouble to bring him some bone buttons he couldn't get in Italy and when I called in to collect the suit I could see he was pleased to see me.

'Why is it – some come out like this?' I asked him in my painful Italian.

'The material, the man, lots of things. I always try my best, the suit always comes good but sometimes,' he held his hands up like a true Roman, 'it just happens. I think it's like everything . . . like a painter, a maestro: all work is good but now and then is one – special.'

He smiled. He'd had his share.

When I brought my suit home it was Sunday lunch-time; on Sundays we didn't have lunch until four o'clock after the pubs turned out. Mum was in the scullery amidst the joint, roast potatoes, veg and Yorkshire pud. This weekly roast was a tall order on our little galvanised gas cooker and Mum hardly had a minute to look at my latest acquisition. Dad came home at about three-thirty. I could see he was in a good mood. He saw me hovering in the kitchen doorway, the suit hanging over one of the four straight-back chairs placed at the table in the middle of the room, its

Sunday position. He put Mum's pint of milk stout on the table and pointed at the suit.

'What's all this then?'

'Oh, it's my new suit, picked it up this morning.'

He lifted it up by the wooden hanger Mr Stevens had given me and turned it round, taking it to the window to see it in better light. The way he held it as he examined the stitching of the lapels made me realise he had never had a tailor-made suit and yet it was obvious he had a real appreciation of good clothes. I remembered how smart he was in his courting photos, in his white on white shirts, on leave during the War.

'Let's see it on you then,' he said, handing me the jacket. I slipped into it. He walked round me, taking in the thumb-tip drape, examining the pitch of the sleeve, running his hand over the collar, snug against the neck. He said, 'Now you're getting good gear you've got to look after it. It's not for lounging around in, you know, nothing knocks out gear quicker. When you get indoors take it off and put yer old stuff on. I've always put my stuff away at night, folded it proper and put it away. No matter how late or under the weather I was.'

He came round to face me. In his expression was pride but there was something else as well – a realisation that his boys were growing up. Perhaps he recognised that a big part of his life was over. No, he'd never had a bespoke suit; probably the best thing he'd ever had was the black Crombie knocked down to thirty bob in Petticoat Lane for his honeymoon. Seeing him looking at me, I wished I could have afforded to buy him a bespoke suit as well. Dad saw me watching him, he pulled his arms into his sides and said in his Cagney voice, 'You look the business, sucker.'

As my evenings spent at the YMCA led to exciting times and new acquaintances, my days at work became dull by comparison. I started travelling to table-tennis competitions all over England and, although I was invariably knocked out in the early rounds, these weekends were always exhilarating. There was a glamour about the events and the people. Of course the best players were idolised and their company sought after, and soon I came into contact with two guys living locally who were highly placed in this order: Ray Dorkin and Bobby Raybold. Bobby was the taller of the pair, with thick blond coxcomb hair, and the kind of golden skin usually found on girls. He was a wonderful player, exciting, erratic; a leftie with the kind of explosive backhand smash even Roy Studd would have envied. It was rumoured that Victor Barna himself had taught Bobby his backhand. He was also extremely flash, and at first I didn't think I would like him much. At an Open Championship being played at Skegness, most of us competitors were billeted in the local Butlin's so lots of high jinks were anticipated behind those famous blue doors. On the first day I saw a girl with the most exquisite legs I had ever laid eyes on. She was wearing the normal playing shorts but they looked very different on her. I couldn't understand why everybody else wasn't weak at the knees. I asked Eddie Hodson, the guy I was standing next to, who she was.

'That's Ruth, Ruth Welsh. She's from Portsmouth.'

'Christ, she's amazing.'

'Yep, she's only got eyes for Ray though. I'd forget it.'

'Ray – who's Ray?'

'Ray Dorkin, he's over there, look, where she's heading.'

'Is he her fella then?'

'No,' said Eddie, who was the same age as me, but looked younger. 'No, she's just nuts about him. I think he's into older women.' Eddie's baby face belied an advanced maturity and he was also one half of a duo known as the terrible twins; he and his doubles partner, Laurie Landry, were the English junior one and two. They were so good that they were already winning events in senior competitions. Eddie filled me in on Ray. He had been one of the best in the country, unequalled as England's leading junior, and later became an Essex regular with a defence so good, so beautiful to watch, that he drew crowds whenever he played. He'd contracted tuberculosis and had been ordered to stop playing for a few years.

'What's he doing here then?' I wanted to know.

'Oh, he just loves ping and of course the girls; they say TB is an afro . . . makes you randy. I'm surprised you don't know him, he comes from East Ham. I'll introduce you.'

That was how I met Ray and consequently the lovely Ruth. I used to look at Ruth's flawless limbs and wonder how Ray resisted. When I got to know him a bit, I asked him.

'I've tried, old chap,' he admitted laconically. 'She throws a good punch and doesn't go the distance – you know, she's a romantic.'

Ray lived just off the Barking Road at the East Ham end in St

Below: Open championship at Filey, 1956

Left: Ray Dorkin and Bobby Raybold

John's Road. He had been taught to play table-tennis by a coach called Wally Reid at a club which was little more than a corrugated-iron hut in the main road just before the Granada cinema. Of an evening we'd look in at the club and Ray would 'knock up' with me, encouraging me to practise my attack, casually returning my best with his fluid defence. He was certainly something to watch. With most defensive players one isn't really aware of a style; they just get the ball back and the one on the attack does all the fireworks, and the usual weakness for a player with a defensive game is when the ball is hit directly at them. I once saw the great Johnny Leach beaten by an opponent who persisted with this kind of attack. (I'm talking about the game before sponge rubber bats came into use. I don't know how it works now.) Ray didn't have this flaw. You could hit the ball at him for hours and he'd just keep chopping it back, every one returned to the base line. What set him apart was the grace which came with his concentration. So many athletes stretched to the full become ungainly with the exertion. An Yvonne Goolagong is rare. So was Ray Dorkin.

Ray worked for a shipping agent in Leadenhall Street and we fell into the habit of having lunch together. I'd usually go to him, as the cafés in his area were a bit more fun, and one day he said Bobby Raybold was joining us at the Tower Hill Lyon's. He reassured me, 'Bob is a Brahma, when you get to know him.' He must have sensed that Bob and I would click; he pushed us together like a Jewish matchmaker, which was quite out of character. Raybold did have glamour, partly from a certain quality in his nature. At first I thought he was just flash, or Harry Nash as we termed it, but I soon discovered he was basically a shy, withdrawn character who had developed this outgoing, rather amoral persona. Bob was also a maverick. I don't know that he had any real friends but he swam in lots of pools, none without good reason. Women, or rather the seduction of women, came high on his list of motivation and he was charming and ruthless. Girls didn't appear to have any deep effect on him, and this seemed to make him a challenge for lots of women.

Late one night in the sitting-room of his parents' corner house in Clacton Road, he confessed that if he could find a successful way to talk to the girls he fancied in the street, his life would be just roses. 'I just can't get started from nowhere. I know guys who can do it, but I can't.'

It was already late and I was contemplating the long walk home, but Bob went to the radiogram and turned over 'Songs for Swinging Lovers'. He seemed set for a discussion. He said he envisaged his life as a caravanserai with endless caravans of ladies pausing to dally and then moving on.

I knew the problem. So many times in the mornings I had sighted tempting creatures, strap-hanging, elegant legs astride to counter the rocking motion, unaware of my gaze in the anonymity of the electric Underground. I had felt the iron bands around my chest as I contemplated intruding on the mysteries behind the vacant expressions.

'Yeah,' I said – I could always jog home – 'I never know how to start, perhaps it's to do with being left-handed and having the right side of the brain developed.'

'Which of your balls is bigger?' said Bob, stretching his fingers. In the glow of the electric fire his hand resembled armour. Frank crooned in the background.

'The left – yeah, the left.'

'You should dress to the left – puts less strain on 'em.'

'I thought you wanted to solve the girl problem. After all, if we reckon women are as sexy as guys, they must be not getting enough.'

'Most of 'em don't, well that's what they tell me. D'ya want a coffee?' He wandered into the kitchen, sliding the door carefully so as not to wake his parents asleep upstairs. I followed. He put some milk into a saucepan and lit the gas under it.

'Do you like this? It's not real coffee,' he said, taking a square bottle of Camp from a cupboard.

'No, it's chicory – I got used to it during the Blitz.' I liked the label. 'I've seen you with girls at tournaments; it doesn't seem a problem.'

'It's only a problem when I really fancy them and I don't know them, but I know what I want to do with them. I go all stiff.'

'In more ways than one, eh Bob?'

We took our cups back into the lounge. Bob stretched out on the divan and I flopped into the matching armchair. I really enjoyed our nocturnal chats. It felt a bit like Holmes and Watson in the Basil Rathbone movies.

'So if you didn't fancy them you'd be all right?'

'Sure, I'm always fine with . . . '

'If I chatted up somebody you had eyes for, then when I got to know her a bit, I could introduce you, all kosher like.'

There was silence from the horizontal Bob. I knew the idea grabbed him. His eyes glinted across the room. I let it sink in for a moment, and added, 'And you could do the same for me.'

'D'ya think you could do it?'

'Well, I can try.'

He hesitated, as if considering whether to divulge a secret.

'Have you ever heard of Eileen Wornham?'

'No.'

'That's somebody I'd really like to meet, she's really something, I can't believe you've never heard of her. There was a gang of minders used to keep an eye on her. It's been really hard to get close to her, I can tell you.'

I was beginning to have doubts about my project. 'What do you mean, minders?'

'Sort of local mob took it on themselves to keep off outsiders.'

'Blimey.'

'Not so much now. I often see her at Upton Park catching the tube. She works up West.'

Bob and I started meeting on the platform every morning. I caught the train at Plaistow, and went one stop down the line where Bob was waiting on the uptown platform. On the third morning he pointed out a small figure with long black hair who was just boarding a non-smoking carriage. He gave me an encouraging wink and I jumped on to the train. That day I just observed. So this was what Bob really liked. It wasn't hard to see why. Eileen was a real corker, a pocket Venus. Her long hair was shiny – 'a silken mass of sheen' as we in advertising would have said. Turned-up nose, big round eyes and a mouth that was a perfect mix of sultriness and innocence. I couldn't really see her body. She changed trains at Charing Cross and caught the Bakerloo Line to Piccadilly Circus. I followed her to Golden Square – Golden Square! – and her shapely ankles walked into the Granada building. It was nine a.m. The next day I got off work a bit early and went to Golden Square and found a bench in the central garden which gave me a good view of the door which Eileen had entered. The flower-beds were packed with wallflowers, laid out like rugs. Their scent was thick. Just before six, when I was thinking I'd blown it, she came out and walked up Regent Street, along Oxford Street and then into Edgware Road. She went into a little cinema just before the Lotus House Chinese Restaurant.

Using my 20/10 vision from the other side of the road, I could see that she didn't go to the box office but showed a card to the usherette who waved her in. She went up the stairs to the circle. I hovered a bit, imagining myself like Gérard Philipe in *The Knave of Hearts*. Then I bought a ticket and went up to the circle. We saw the film together, her outlined against the screen in the front row, me in the back row. On Friday morning I was up early enough to get to Upton Park by the time she came down the stairs. She was wearing a mustard coat. I hit on her while we waited for the train. I was surprisingly relaxed.

'Are you Eileen?'

She looked at me; her face registered that she didn't know me. 'Yes.'

'Are you Eileen Wornham?' I sort of dragged it out a bit. In close-up her eyes were something to write home about.

'Yes,' she said tentatively, as though expecting bad news.

I did an exaggerated look round. 'I don't see any bodyguards.' Then I lowered my voice. 'I heard you never travelled alone. Are you sure you're Eileen Wornham?'

She laughed, showing nice small teeth. 'You heard, did you, and who did you hear from?'

'Oh, loads of guys, all desperate to make your acquaintance but they never catch you alone. I wasn't sure it was you but it seemed too good an opportunity to miss. Hope you don't mind?'

'No – not really,' she said as the train came in. We strap-hung to Mansion House and I got out. I discovered she worked as a secretary for a company that owned amongst others the Granada near where she lived in Abbotts Road, and that she had an employee's pass which let her and a friend into any of their chain of cinemas once a week. We agreed to look out for one another on the train.

That evening I reported to Bob, who was delighted and impressed. The next day we went out trying to find a jacket suitable for him to wear for his introduction. He settled for a model which was in the window of Charkam's, opposite the Astoria in the Charing Cross Road. It was a proper eye-catcher, a two-button drape with patch pockets, made of a soft fabric almost like a vicuna, probably a cashmere mix. The only thing I wasn't sure about was the colour, the palest of powder-blues. Not that he didn't look amazing, but I associated that kind of blue with innocence, which clashed a bit with Bob's intent. Perhaps Eileen wouldn't be perturbed by the wolf in lamb's-wool.

After carriage-hopping and changing trains looking for Eileen, I bumped into her on the train coming home. She invited me to her house on Saturday afternoon. I asked Bob if it would be a good idea for us both to arrive; I'd dropped in on him en route home. He thought I'd better go by myself this time.

'It's just tea,' he said.

'Tea can lead to anything; that's the one good thing about being English,' I said.

I went for tea. To my surprise she was in the house alone. We sat in the front room. It wasn't a front room like ours, unused with just lino on the floor and no furniture, but calm and carpeted, with sofas. Sunlight shafted through the lace curtains. You could hear the roar from West Ham playing at home in the distance. She played some records on her gramophone and then she put on a record called 'John and Marcia' which she said 'would make me laugh'. It was a 78, the likes of which I had never heard; the voices of a man and a woman repeating each other's names with increasing fervour. Eileen giggled throughout. She sat on the settee opposite me with her legs pulled up beside her, her loose hair almost reaching the hand she used to support herself. With her caramel eyes she looked like some wonderful cat. I kept wishing I wasn't on a mission. I had the urge to go and sit close to her, fondle her hair. It occurred to me that I'd better introduce Bob soon.

He looked terrific the evening we waited on the Mile End platform. It was years before the English really let loose with colour, and Bob in his dashing jacket definitely stood out from the other commuters. I thought how well a pair of royal-blue suede casuals would have finished off his outfit, but we hadn't even heard of Elvis, let alone his shoes. I spotted Eileen in her usual carriage and we squeezed in, Bob taking a final puff on his Senior Service and dropping it on the platform. It all went smoothly enough and I nipped out at Plaistow, leaving them to travel on together to Upton Park and get to know one another. It didn't work though, and I never did find out the reason why. Bob said he felt he wasn't her type; he'd asked her out but she hedged. I thought he could have taken it a bit slower myself. When I was rehearsing *Alfie* in New York for my Broadway début in '64, I received a note from Eileen at the stage door and consequently I took her out for coffee. We chatted a bit about the old times in East Ham and I was dying to know whether she would have purred if I'd stroked her hair that Saturday afternoon. But, as she was happily married and living in New York, it seemed a bit indelicate.

Miss Robbins at Wilkes Bros announced one morning that we had to vacate Friday House and a new location in Oxford Street had been found. Although it meant further to travel, I was pleased.

It was right in the West End and I'd begun to notice that the girls who used the Central Line were definitely the most glamorous. It also sent that alarm clock off in my head, reminding me that time was passing, and slowly but surely my life was changing. Like a ship which alters course a few degrees unnoticed, but can run adrift of its destination by hundreds of miles. That lunch-time I sat in a little garden under the only tree in Cheapside and tried to think out my next move.

I didn't like the advertising game much. I hadn't met anybody I'd taken to, and I was still only a glorified messenger boy. I was haunted by the neatly written statement on my birth certificate where my dad's profession had been given as milliner's packer. The most appealing part of my job was wandering about town on errands, discovering the secrets of London, travelling on the greatest of British inventions, the open-ended double decker, with its arcane routes. Nobody at Wilkes Bros was itching to promote me and it was obvious I would have to instigate any upward movement. I would get to the top of the tree and see the view from there. I couldn't think of anything else to do.

Using the projected move of the office as an excuse, I reorganised the filing system so that nobody could find anything if I wasn't in the office. Within a fortnight, an OAP called Mr Appleby was assigned as a messenger and took over my tobacco box. I started hanging out with Bas and Glyn in the studio. Glyn was the artist and a part-time drummer. Bas often came in hung over and grumpy but after lunch and a 'livener', as my dad called it, was rosy-cheeked and expansive. He let me watch him doing his 'visualising'. By the time we transferred to 299 Oxford Street, I had concocted my own specimen book. Using Bas's excellent designs and slogans, I worked back from the finished print, making a tracing original in my own hand. I invested in a sturdy brown-paged book, sticking the glossy on the right-hand page and my mark-up opposite it. I took what I thought was a good cross-section from the files and half filled the book, sign-writing my name complete with middle initial on the front, and under it VISUALISER – TYPOGRAPHER. My old English calligraphy was paying off at last!

There was a weekly advertising magazine whose ads on the back pages were scanned regularly by insecure ad men who felt their jobs to be at risk. A firm with a Regent telephone number was looking for an 'adventurous typographer'. As our new number at Wilkes Bros was the Langham exchange, I thought this might be 'just the job' for me. For the uninitiated, a visualiser usually dreams up the ad from scratch, giving precise indications where the headings and copy should be. The copy is written by the copywriter and it is the job of the typographer to adjust this information to fit into the space visualised. He does this by counting the characters and choosing the typeface size and spacing, so the bumf can be easily read in the space designated. It is then sent off to an engraver who sets it up and if it is correct makes the metal block used for printing. Being an exact science involving the barest mathematics – although there were lots of esoteric discussions about the harmonics between the shape and personality of the typeface and the product being unloaded on the public – and as the compositor only held about a dozen full sets of variations, the choice between sports cars and ladies' woollen undies didn't seem to warrant studying the many books I was encouraged to read on the subject. I had no fears about holding the job down. Getting it was the problem.

As it was the Fifties and pre-wizkid fashion, I was self-conscious about being only seventeen. I had to look mature enough for the question of age not to arise. I considered a hat, but Dad's trilbies wouldn't go anywhere near my $7\frac{1}{8}$-inch head, and also I couldn't keep it on during the interview, though I thought I might carry it like a prop. I'd seen an actor at Fairbairn use one to great effect. This had me thinking about make-up, and I did some experiments at home but the drawn-on wrinkles just looked like warpaint in normal light. What did work was a brown and maroon mix rubbed right into the skin directly under the eyes. My dad had a light tweed overcoat which I suppose had started life as a Raglan; on me it resembled a short, loose tent but it did give an outlandish look in much the same way as a cloak does. Having made up my eyes in the Oxford Circus public convenience, and wearing as a last-minute prop a pair of specs which I'd found lying around the office, I turned up for my interview at one-fifteen. The agency was called Napper, Stinton and Wooley and occupied an entire rather nondescript modern building in Great Chapel Street. I was shown into the office of a guy who had the account executive uniform on; grey suit, stiff collar and tie. He stood up; we shook hands. He indicated a chair, I put my specimen book on his desk and sat down. I took my specs off in order to see a bit better.

'Well, Mr . . . ' he looked at my script-written name on the book, 'Stamp.'

I smiled.

'I see you are a visualiser typographer. You know the vacant post is for a typographer. Pure and simple.'

That had worked. I said, 'I've been a bit dry lately. I thought a change might be as good as a rest.' I'd overheard Mr Baker unload some work on to Shylock using that dry bit.

'Let's have a look at your work, shall we?'

'Let's.' I put the specs back on and moved round to his side of the desk, alongside him, so I could look over the lenses unnoticed.

'Hmm,' he said, 'where did you train?'

'Oh, St Martin's and – er – Bolt Court,' I replied. The St Martin's bit was a lie. I had attended two evening classes at Bolt Court which had been more boring than school, both about the lives of guys who'd invented the types named after them.

But he was obviously impressed by the contents of 'my book', and I thought I might have gone a bit over the top when he said, 'This unfortunately isn't a senior post we are hoping to fill.'

I moved back round to my seat. He closed the book and pushed it across to my side of the desk. I took my specs off and placed them facing him on the book. I figured, well I've blown this one, I'll just hang in as long as I can and get the experience.

'What sort of salary did you have in mind?'

I had originally planned to double my wages every time I changed my job. As I was now earning £4 a week at Wilkes Bros, I figured I'd ask for £8, but I heard myself saying, 'Seven hundred and fifty,' which worked out at £15 a week.

'Yes.' He tampered with his small, tightly knotted tie. 'As I said, unfortunately it is not a senior position.'

'That is unfortunate,' I said.

'We could only go to £500.'

I leaned forward and took the specs off the book and put them in my pocket. I then sat still and softly took a deep breath. He got a cigarette out of a silver box on the desk and lit it with a desk lighter. He didn't offer me one. I reached forward, took my book and put it on my lap. I remember thinking, this is great, it's just like being in a play without rehearsing. He was looking at his nails which were short and clean. So I stood up.

He said, 'I suppose we could go to £12.10 a week.'

'Do you need to show my book to anybody else?'

'No, no, my decision is sufficient – have we a deal?'

'I have to give notice – I can start in a fortnight.' I was anxious to get out, suddenly worried about the make-up I hadn't bothered to powder, but he insisted on taking me up to the fourth floor to show me the airy studio where I would be working, past corridors with edgy secretaries zipping about. Suddenly I was back on the street. I had done it. It was unreal. I could feel a kind of energy throbbing through my body. I walked across Soho; everything looked startlingly clear and bright. I saw a street clock saying one-thirty. One-thirty! The whole thing had taken just fifteen minutes.

All of my career in the ad game was a bit like that. I carried on changing jobs and increasing my wages. In general, by the time it sifted through to the accounts department that correction charges from the engravers were a bit higher than normal, I had sussed the job. Looking back at those years, my inability to consume booze probably gave me an edge in the world of advertising. I left the game for good in 1956; a thousand-a-year man.

Thirteen

IN RACING TRIM

Above: Stan Jones, born in Scorpio 1928

In Racing Trim

Shortly after starting my new job, I ran into Stan Jones. I met him at the YMCA. I had continued to mooch around the four floors, even though Bernie Wilson and his family had moved back North, and I had failed to gain an Essex place at the County trials. I still played ping and it was a terrific place to hang out; I was trying to interest a brunette called Lillian Eisenhower. The club also had regular dances and concerts. One evening, when the hall they used for the concerts was being made ready, one of the seniors, a woman in her late twenties, was sitting on her haunches fixing a makeshift curtain to the front of the stage. Frankly, she had the best rear end I had seen since Grace and I was transfixed. She was a statuesque type and her putty-coloured gabardine skirt was under some stress.

A voice behind me said, 'Great bottle, isn't it?' I turned and saw Stan. I felt a bit embarrassed. He grinned. 'It's even better close up.'

'Do you know her then?'

'Yeah, she's my regular,' he said, still grinning at my consternation.

'I – er – hope I haven't . . . '

'Don't be a burke, there's more than one slice to a cake.'

I knew who Stan was, of course; I'd heard gossip about his impressive girlfriend and his exploits, but my time at the club had been spent almost exclusively in the basement with the table-tennis jocks. He was ten years older which made it unlikely that our paths would cross, so I was flattered when he seemed to know about me and offered to introduce me to the crouching beauty.

'I hope you'll come to the show Saturday. Stan's going to sing,' she said. I did and Stan and I became mates.

It was quirky that Stan chose me as a hobbady. It wasn't even a case of a teacher choosing a pupil. He treated me as an equal, younger, but equal. His face in repose resembled a sharp Leslie Howard, even to the high forehead and ash-coloured curly hair, but once he grinned, laughed or spoke he instantly resembled the Joker in *Superman* comics. He was a docker when we teamed up. Although he'd been to sea and spent years as an 'iron fighter', he'd remained single and lived in Holborn Road with his mum and stepfather. Marlon Brando's publicity image – 'the face of a poet and the body of a gladiator' – also fitted Stan. He usually saw Lilly (all the Lillys I've met have been lookers) one or two nights a week and we quickly fell into the habit of spending the other five

together. I really didn't know what he saw in me. He could
certainly sing, but at the concert he seemed tense and the voice
didn't reflect his gleeful outlook on life. I figured he'd crack it
sooner or later. He stood up and did it, which counted for a lot in
my book. He had a motorbike, a Matchless; he taught me how to
ride pillion and the world became my oyster.

Most young guys are naturally horny in the years when the
hormone rushes start, and Stan was no exception; he just seemed
to get a bigger rush than most. We made forays to dances and pubs
in Epping, Rainham, Woodford and the haunts of other outlying
clusters of 'class crumpet', as he put it. Stan never tried to seduce
or even take home on the first night the girls he met. He had a
'stacking system' so there was always one girl who felt the time was
right to move on him. During late nights at the Tabu in Plashet
Grove (our first local coffee bar), we sipped chocolate-topped
cappuccinos from Pyrex cups, listened to Buddy Holly, discussed
everything in general and girls in particular. The painted black
walls and flashing jukebox became as familiar to me as my own
home. It was the first place I could go and sit and feel really comfy.
Stan had a zest which seemed to come from not being tied to any
post, either moral or conceptual. He was what we called 'fly', the
only word I know combining the two Yiddish words *hutzpah* and
nous. Although the jokes he told and the things he said were often
coarse, nobody ever took offence. I found a lot of my early fears
vanishing as his attitude of seeing things without garnish filtered
through to me.

On my encounter with Horobin and the doubts about my
success with girls, Stan said, 'Nothing wrong with the occasional
iron.' He always called gays irons (iron hoof – pouf) or ginger
beers. 'You know, in the Navy guys used to pay, to go down on me,
pay *me*. It was great, 'specially the old salts. I'd make 'em take their
teeth out, of course.' A wicked laugh always followed these
disclosures.

I told him of Grace, the loss, the worry that perhaps so many
orgasms before ejaculation might have damaged my pistol. He
thought that was terrific, she must have been a real blinder –
'Before you could come, eh?' He told me about his first orgasm, in
the Imperial picture house at Silvertown. A girl he had sat next to
in the dark gave him a sweet and let him squeeze her breasts.

'The next thing I knew she had my strides open and was jackin' me off. I shot over everything. Thought I'd done myself a mischief.' He laughed. 'That first time – yeah! Sometimes I force myself to go without to get that first-time thrill again, and I often get 'em to turn over – it's really rude.'

Stan could go on for hours with sexual theory. 'I like girls who like it,' he once said to me.

'I thought they all did,' I replied lamely.

'Naah! Girls ain't like us, you know, they don't come every time, lots don't come ever.' Seeing I wasn't totally convinced, he continued, 'When I was doing my *Lady* massages [he'd run an ad in *Lady* magazine, very successfully] I came across a lot, not virgins, married, but had never got off. Amazing, ain't it?'

'Why, though?'

'A lot of blokes are just one-rub merchants, most of 'em just don't realise the bird has to get off as well. After all, there ain't no dictionary word for what girls shoot over you. It's not . . . '

'Acknowledged.'

He grinned. 'I do – I've had my short and curlies full of it more times than you've had hot dinners.'

'It's not just gleet? I get a lot of that,' I said.

'No, no. Gleet's from the prostate; this is thick, white. It's not as jellified as ours, though.'

He'd obviously been deep into the subject. I just smiled encouragement. I was a dry sponge for this level of griff.

'It's funny how curious about crumpet guys are – well, I am. I remember the first girl I took indoors, she wouldn't have the light on. I was so set on seeing what it looked like, I took her into the kitchen and lit the stove. "To keep us warm." I couldn't see much that time though.'

'But if they're married, you'd think the wife would say something – if she's not getting off.' I wanted to get round to his technique.

'A lot of birds don't know, actually don't know. The ones who know, and can't, don't want to admit it, even to their mates. I had a bird once, a mannequin. She'd had a couple of boyfriends but I was the first who did it for her. I thought she was getting heavy vapours, almost passed out. The next morning I found her writing her mum a note, telling her what it was like. The mum had never had it either. Talking of mums, I don't see how you can have a good kid without both parents really enjoying it.' He paused, as if considering his insight.

I said, 'Well, I suppose if you don't get the feeling, you wouldn't be keen to do it, with the risk an' all.'

'Sure. Why have some dirty soapy bastard like me banging away? I don't enjoy it with girls who use it like a gadget. They never get off, they're so busy impressing you how great they are at it and then there's the price for the use of . . . '

'How d'ya know which won't enjoy it?'

'It's just a feeling. The other night I took that bird we met at the Ilford Palais out to dinner. As soon as we got sat down she asked me for cigarettes, not a cigarette, a packet. Called the waiter. Twenty Craven A. She giggled, put them in her bag. I thought, no. Nothing in her gadget tonight. Not mine any rate! Too expensive. Too pre . . . you know.'

'Premeditated?'

I never thought he would get married. I couldn't imagine the girl who would be as fly as him, or a set of circumstances he couldn't cope with by himself. I was wrong, even though I was there at the very onset and didn't spot it, or maybe I just didn't want to. Stan's regular girlfriend suddenly gave him the air. She'd met a fella who wanted to marry her. Stan was philosophical. 'You can't beat that!' he said. 'You can't compete with a bloke who offers marriage. It's like cheating at cards!' It meant he was suddenly on the loose at weekends. As if in celebration, he sold his Matchless, feather-bed frame and all. A black Lea-Francis Sports 14 replaced it. I saw it on my way to the club, parked outside his house, looking really saucy, with the hood already down. 'In racing trim,' he called it. I can't tell what zest that car added to my life.

Practically the only cars I had ever been in were either wedding or funeral transport. This was a real hairy sports car; just to hear its roar as we barrelled through the Blackwall Tunnel, with the slipstream whipping my hair over my eyes, was a thrill I wanted never to end. Stan was just as chuffed as me, screaming past bikers and shouting abuse as he racing-changed into top gear. Our destinations were almost inconsequential and became farther and farther afield as we sought to prolong the journey.

Stan confessed he'd always wanted a different name but it had obviously not occurred to him to do anything about it. To me it presented no problem. I said, 'Just change it. Call yourself whatever you like and tell everybody you meet from now on your new name.'

He didn't have an idea about what name he wanted, and I could see he felt self-conscious. I made it easy. 'Look, your name is Stan.'

'Stanley,' he said.

I had a sudden flash and said, 'OK, how about Lee? You've had twenty-eight years as Stan, now you've progressed to Lee – Lee with the Lea-Francis.' I could see he loved it. I said, 'OK, Lee, let's go for a drive and tell some new folks your name.'

We were suited up that Saturday evening and drove to a manor hall out Chigwell way. The ballroom was next door to a big pub called the Bald Hinde with a lavish private bar and a bar billiards table in the middle. Stan ordered me a lager and lime which was about all I could handle, and I kept calling him by his new name to get him used to it. I had never seen him so buoyant. I felt I had opened a door for him. He seemed to have a new perspective as we commandeered the billiards; he was talking about leaving the docks, explaining to me how they'd been getting away with murder for years and how it had to end soon. Some Argentine sailors he'd

Above: Lee in the Lea-Francis

met had called him Rubio because he was so blond, and asked him to go back to Argentina with them. 'A man who looks like you could make a fortune there. Every woman will go crazy for your hair and your white skin. And eat, you eat meat, three times a day, but what meat, not shit like you eat here.' He babbled on; people from the dance came into the pub.

I said, 'I've always had the feeling you can do what you like with your life. It's only just becoming clear about the price of the ticket.'

Stan, or Lee as he now was, said, 'I'd love to be a singer – with a band. I can't see how to start, but I've got to get out of the docks first.'

Had I been able to hold more booze, we might never have gone to the dance but Lee, noticing my glass was empty, said, 'Let's drift in with these people, they've got passes.'

The half-time records were just finishing as we successfully jibbed in and stood around taking stock as the band came on to the stage. Lee spotted a girl almost straight away and took off to get a dance. He could do all the ballroom stuff and was confident even when the floor was almost bare. Unlike myself. I'd still only mastered 'the Creep'. So I was confined to one or two excursions an evening. Three or four dances went by, so I assumed that either he was doing well – having a 'dry run' as he called it – or I'd just lost him in the crush. Then I spotted him with two girls standing to one side. He beckoned me over and it was obvious which of the girls had taken his fancy. She was tall and at first glance impervious. The friend was a bow-wow. Lee introduced us.

Our eyes met, as they say. Tall and impervious gave me a curious look. It was a look I'd only seen at the movies and then between women. The wings of her hair were highlighted, pulled back severely and gathered behind her head, leaving her face un-adorned. The face was oval and perfect, lacking only that element of caricature that cartoonists are so fond of. Her body was wonderful; she could have been a Vargas girl if she hadn't been so tall. I didn't know why I wasn't fancying her myself – I'd yet to hit that period of being drawn to girls who gave me a hard time. A waltz started. Stan 'gathered her in his arms' and one-two-three'd on to the dancing area. I saw that glow between them for a moment before they were lost amongst the other dancers, a mutual belonging which adds a dimension to a couple whether they are plain or beautiful.

The bow-wow was eyeing me with a 'would you like to fall in love as well' look. I said something facetious like, 'I'll look this one out,' and moved off to watch the band. It is easy to give Fate the credit when it is pushing you in a direction where you want to go; much harder to be optimistic when life appears to be giving you a bitter pill. That was my condition as I realised my first adult mate was driving his Lea-Francis in another direction and I wasn't even in the jump seat.

Lee took his new friend up West for a night out the following weekend. On Monday evening he told me they had checked in overnight at a hotel in Craven Street, next to Charing Cross Station. He didn't go into the usual detailed erotica, but the expression on his face and his comment, 'She's so rude, so rude!' told me he'd met his match. More and more the car would be missing from its spot outside his house as I passed on my way to the club or the pictures. Some nights I'd hear the sporty toot of his hooter outside 124 and we'd zoom off to the Tabu, or to the Chinese café next to the Co-op at East Ham. He started giving me names of 'girls he'd done', local girls who continued to knock on his door whenever he was in and his folks weren't. I was amazed. With one or two exceptions they were all in the butter-wouldn't-melt-in-the-mouth department. Armed with this inside info, I took a fresh look at these schoolgirl violets and my own soirée musicals in the Rec. and the hills beyond became quite frequent.

I stayed in a lot of nights. Our new television was still a novelty; watching it I saw just how bad a lot of English working actors were and started thinking again about trying to act myself, commenting on duff performances when I saw them. One evening I complained, 'I could do better than that myself.' It wasn't the first time I'd made this remark aloud. The TV was positioned for our one socket and temperamental aerial more than from any aesthetic consideration, which meant that whoever was watching the flickering black and white screen sat around the dining table as though at a meal, with the Ferguson twelve-inch as an absorbing guest. My dad, present on this occasion, and obviously feeling he'd better nip this anomaly in the bud, said, 'People like us don't do things like that!' It was said with such quiet finality that Chris, who had his whole face in an orange, looked up to see what he'd missed. I opened my mouth more in automatic response than anything else, but Tom, whose steady eyes were still on me, continued, 'Just don't talk about it any

Above: Me in my Dayton roll

more. I don't want you to even think about it!' He didn't say it
unkindly. In retrospect I'm sure he felt he was saving me a lot of
heartache. I never spoke about it again.

Coming home from work one evening, I ran into Bob Raybold.
He and a few mates were going to see this new actor in a film at the
Coronation, Romford Road. The film was called *East of Eden*. He
leaned on me a bit to go, saying a boy called David Baxter would be
there and I might get off on him. 'He's a bit of a Bohemian, always
wears a duffel coat.'

I don't know why I didn't go. I was feeling depressed a lot of the
time and I'd started to worry about my National Service which had
already snapped up most of the lads a bit older than myself.
Anyway, I passed on Bob's invitation, which just goes to show what
you can miss by feeling sorry for yourself, but I made a mental note
of the film's title.

Waiting for a bus at the Boleyn a few nights later, I had just
decided to leg it when an almost empty number 15 came along and
I went upstairs and took the back seat. These seats still had a
padded arm-rest which struck me as a touch of luxury and I always
used them when vacant.

The only other passenger was sitting a few seats in front of me.
His astrakhan hair looked familiar. It was Roy Studd enjoying his
last smoke of the day. I joined him. He was coming home from
his girlfriend's, who he said had packed him off home because he
was boring. I figured she must have had a very low boredom
threshold.

'What are you up to then, Roy?'

'In the RAF. I'm doing my time in Hong Kong. Fly out next
week.'

I felt a kind of melancholy and, as always, a sense of time
passing. Studd in the Airforce and off to the Orient, the end of an
era. I remembered my Granny Kate's admonition, 'When a door
closes, a window opens.' Her feisty optimism didn't lift my spirits
on that night. It seemed that when one door closed behind me,
another smashed right in my face.

Prince Regent's Lane was deserted. I walked up the hill which
incorporated the sewage outfall. We didn't think of it as a sewer as
it was all sealed in with a grassy verged track running along the top
of the pipe to the Thames at Woolwich. I had always intended to
walk that path all the way to the river, yet, with my eighteenth

birthday only months away and boyhood over, it was one of a heap of things I hadn't got around to.

I looked east along the rise. It was lit only by a new moon like a dish, thin as a sixpence, angled as if to catch the single star falling towards it.

COMING ATTRACTIONS

In the next volume Terence forsakes his old haunts and friends and is drawn up West to method acting evening classes. Unbeknownst to his family, he entangles himself in the forbidden world of showbiz. Drained by this double life, he takes the plunge and leaves home. Things don't get easier – until, at the fag-end of the Fifties, he decides to go for it . . .